AWAKENING THE HEART

Awakening the Heart

First edition, Paperback

Cultivating Connections Press

www.cultivatingconnectionsvt.com

ISBN: 979-8-9953084-0-9

Library of Congress Control Number: 2026906858

Printed in the United States of America

To the one who went first—thank you.

TABLE OF CONTENTS

"When I was a young man, I wanted to change the world. I found it was difficult to change the world, so I tried to change my nation. When I found I couldn't change the nation, I began to focus on my town. I couldn't change the town, and as an older man, I tried to change my family.

Now, as an old man, I realize the only thing I can change is myself, and suddenly I realize that if long ago I had changed myself, I could have made an impact on my family. My family and I could have made an impact on our town. Their impact could have changed the nation, and I could indeed have changed the world."

— Unknown Monk

Preface

Everybody has a right to define their own recovery and what recovery means to them. For something so deeply personal, it's often spoken about in rigid, universal terms, as if there's a single path, a correct way to arrive, a standard that can be applied to every person. But recovery isn't a formula. It's an experience, and no two experiences are the same.

Society places labels on what recovery should look like. It tends to divide it into what is acceptable and what is not, what is "real" recovery and what is dismissed or questioned. There is a tendency to measure recovery from the outside, by appearance, by method, or by adherence to a specific model, rather than by the internal reality of the person living it. Because of that, people often feel pressured to fit into a version of recovery that was never built for them.

I know that some people would disagree with the path that I walked. Some would say it wasn't the right way, or that it didn't align with what recovery is supposed to be. That perspective assumes there is only one definition that holds truth. It overlooks the fact that what matters most is not how recovery looks from the outside, but whether it creates real change on the inside.

Recovery, at its core, is about freedom. Freedom from the patterns, dependency and suffering that once controlled someone's life. If it truly leads to freedom, then it has meaning regardless of whether it fits into someone else's expectations. Recovery should be self-defined. Not because structure or guidance has no value, but because no one else can fully understand what it takes for another person to come back to themselves.

This book is ultimately larger than my own recovery. The experiences that reshaped my life, particularly those rooted in plant medicine, ritual, and community, made it impossible for me to ignore how access to healing is not evenly distributed. I didn't arrive at this understanding through ideology, but through survival. I know firsthand what it feels like to be dismissed, criminalized, and misunderstood because of perceived mental states. I also know how transformative it is to be met instead with curiosity, respect, and support from people who have walked similar paths.

Expanding access to plant medicines and community-based healing does not come from theory. It comes from witnessing what happens when people are trusted with their own healing under the guidance of care, structure, and peer support. The most meaningful support I've known did not come from authority, but from proximity, from people who could say, "I've been there," and mean it. Peer support is not a lesser form of care, it is a form of healing born from lived experience. Ending discrimination and oppression based on mental health labels requires us to move away from fear and towards connection, away from punishment and towards acceptance. This book is part of that offering, not a guide, but an invitation to imagine a world where healing is treated as a human right, and where those who have survived are allowed to lead.

I remember sitting in rooms where people like me were talked about instead of talked with, and where our stories were reduced to diagnoses, risk factors, and compliance issues. At the same time, I was finding stability and clarity by learning about peer support and plant medicine work that existed outside those systems, guided by people with lived experience rather than authority alone. The contrast was impossible to ignore. In one setting, I was treated as a liability to be managed and in the other, I was treated as a human being capable of responsibility and healing. That difference, between being controlled and being trusted, changed the course of my life. It's why I believe so strongly that access to community-based healing and peer support isn't a fringe idea, it's a matter of human rights and the future of mental health treatment.

This isn't just my story. Our society is currently in the middle of a recovery evolution, and something is shifting in how we treat addiction and mental health. My story is not merely about addiction and drugs. It's a story about mental health, identity, and the responsibility of living.

This book is a work of memoir based on my lived experiences and personal reflections. While every effort has been made to portray events truthfully, some names and identifying details have been changed to protect the privacy of individuals. The perspectives shared here reflect my understanding of these events at the time of writing. Memory is imperfect. This account represents my sincere attempt to make meaning of experiences that shaped my life.

My intention in telling this story is not to present a universal path, but to honestly describe the journey through addiction, self-discovery, and healing as I lived it. The experiences described in this book are not intended as medical or therapeutic guidance, but as personal reflections on a journey of recovery and transformation.

To Mom and Dad

PART I

FOUNDATION

Chapter 1

The Root

Vermont is quiet, but it isn't soft. It sharpens people. It hands them winters that require resilience, forests that demand respect, and communities that remember everything you've ever said or done, for better or worse.

I was raised in that landscape, where mountains sit like old witnesses and rivers carve through stone slowly, patiently, the way transformation works on the human spirit. The culture itself left marks on me long before addiction ever did: the way neighbors show up without needing to ask for permission, the silence of snow at 5 a.m, the sacredness of fire, of woodsmoke, of long drives through dark backroads. This lends to the understanding that nature isn't decoration, it's a force, a teacher, and sometimes a warning.

My family lived inside that environment: intense, intellect-driven, emotionally powerful, unafraid to confront hard truths, and unwilling to live a simple life. My father's mind, my mother's steadfastness, and my siblings' sheer capability and force of personality, everything around me said, "We do not live lightly here."

My parents moved to Vermont in 1988, and by 1992, I had entered the picture as the third of four children. We were an average middle-class family who lived in a rural area and spent a lot of time outside, in nature, exploring and having fun. We were an active athletic family participating in many sports, primarily hockey. Despite having hectic schedules, we always made time for family dinner. Honesty, respect for others, and sticking up for one another were expectations that were woven into daily life. My parents valued and taught us the importance of individual growth, good education, creativity, and caring for others and the environment. A significant challenge growing up in this environment was the lack of socialization with kids my own age. Until the age of nine, when we moved into town, the majority of my early childhood was spent with my family.

Thinking back to my childhood, I had difficult relationships with my older siblings. Brendan was the oldest, and Brianna was next in line. Both of them tried to guide me and my younger brother, Ryan, but it often came across as telling us what to do. I looked up to them and sought their approval, but no matter how hard I tried, I could never get any recognition.

The atmosphere of my home taught me that emotion is real, struggle is real, and potential is real. Nothing was dismissed. Nothing was trivial. Even silence had weight, and because of that, I learned early that identity is not simply who I am, it is also what I come from.

The Vermont winters taught me to withstand challenges. The forests taught me to listen. The family dinners taught me to speak honestly, or not at all. The small-town culture taught me the burden and gift of reputation. The land taught me that transformation is slow, like thawing, like changing seasons, like sediment becoming stone.

By the time addiction entered my life, the seed that would later save me had already been sown. By the time awakening came, the roots were already deep. By the time the ritual formed, the tree had already sprouted, yet the fruit was still seasons away.

This was the first version of me, the one addiction buried and life would later ask me to reclaim.

This is where my story truly begins.

Chapter 2

The Gift of Sensitivity

As a boy, I often felt things before I understood them. I could walk into a room and sense the unspoken tension between people. I noticed who felt comfortable and who didn't, who carried confidence and who carried something heavier. At the time, I thought everyone experienced the world this way. In hindsight, I can see that I was walking into those rooms carrying something I didn't yet understand: my sensitivity. Sensitivity without guidance can feel less like a gift and more like something we need to hide. When something is hidden long enough, we can forget its purpose. When we don't understand what we're carrying, the world has a way of teaching us to hide it.

For most of my life, I believed addiction was simply who I was. It wasn't something I questioned or examined. It was an identity that seemed to explain everything about me. Only years later did I begin to realize that what I had accepted as identity might actually have been something else entirely: a pattern learned in response to pain, disconnection, and a search for relief. I did not understand that identity can change.

Addiction didn't begin with drugs. It began much earlier, in the ways I learned to disconnect from myself. At the time, I thought I was adapting to the world around me. In hindsight, I realize I was slowly becoming someone else . . . before my first heartbreak at fourteen . . . before my best friend's death by suicide . . . before my spine-breaking car accident at eighteen . . . before heroin . . . before the overdose . . . before ayahuasca . . . before I began the search for my identity. Before any of this, there was simply an overly sensitive young boy. Some children move through the world softly, absorbing everything around them. They notice the tone in a voice before the words, the tension in a room. Sensitivity like this can feel almost like a sixth sense. Adults sometimes recognize it first, the way a child listens closely, reads people instinctively, or carries the emotions of others without understanding why.

As a child, I didn't experience this as anything unusual. It simply felt like the way the world worked. Sensitivity gave me awareness, intuition, and an easy connection with others. But gifts that arrive without guidance can also carry a hidden weight. When a young person feels everything deeply, the world can become overwhelming long before they have the tools to deal with it.

Sensitivity is strange that way. It is both a gift and a burden. The same awareness that allows someone to feel the beauty and depth of life can also leave them vulnerable to its pain. Without guidance, many sensitive people spend years trying to escape the very thing that could have been their salvation. The gift of sensitivity that allowed me to feel the world so vividly would later leave me vulnerable to forces I didn't yet understand. I therefore learned early to seek ways to ameliorate the painful sensory overload.

Most men don't understand the gift of sensitivity. We knowingly and intentionally act to disguise it. What many of us never realize is that the very feelings we try to bury are often the key to finding our identity.

Chapter 3

Into the Fall

Before I ever learned what it meant to lose myself, there was death. I was very young, four years old when the world first revealed that it could take things away.

I went hiking with my family to Moss Glenn Falls, a place people speak of with the kind of reverence reserved for beauty and danger intertwined. The water carved its way through ancient stone. I remember the sound of it, rushing that feels like it's speaking directly to your bones.

It was evening, the kind of Vermont summer twilight where the air thins, and the colors shift from gold to something colder. My dad looked out over the gorge and said, calmly, almost academically, "Someone could be pushed off this cliff, into the rushing waters, and die." Then, a passing hiker added, "A woman was murdered here just a few years ago." They were just adults talking, but to me, at that age, those words weren't information. They were an invasion. I sensed the fear in my mom, and it compounded the fear in me. Something inside me broke open.

I don't remember leaving the waterfall. I don't remember the car ride home. Everything after those words was swallowed in a blankness, as if my mind turned its face away from the world to protect me from something too large to understand. The next thing I remember is darkness, coldness, and absolute terror.

I was curled in a ball against the cherry-wood cabinets, crying without sound, my body shaking as though the floor beneath me were alive. My family sat at the dinner table talking softly, eating, unaware that the universe had split open inside me. My mother came to me, touched my shoulder, and asked what was wrong. But how does a child describe a feeling older than language? How does a four-year-old say, something followed me home that wasn't here before?

My mother tucked me into bed, smoothing the blankets as if order could soften whatever had begun inside me. The moment the lights went out, the nightmare awoke fully. I started hearing voices. Voices of people who sounded lost, frightened, begging from distances I couldn't measure. I wasn't imagining monsters. I was hearing the echoes of something ancient, something hollowed-out and human. I was hearing the voice of the recently strangled woman. Then the ceiling changed. I watched the entire universe begin to coalesce above my head, particles swirling, matter forming and collapsing. I felt myself dissolve and expand in the same breath. I had been placed inside the engine of creation and destruction, forced to witness scale far beyond comprehension. Everything felt impossibly large and impossibly small at the same time. The fear of impermanence paled in the face of infinity.

I didn't have the language then, but I know now, a veil was lifted that night. Not in a beautiful way. In a way that left a crack running through me. Children are unable to repress death the way adults do. That night was my first encounter with something so absolute. It planted something in me, a vulnerability, a void, that would shape the years ahead in ways I couldn't possibly understand until much later.

Truth is, we don't fall into addiction randomly. We fall through pre-existing fractures. A four-year-old boy staring into the infinite, feeling the universe breathe above him, learning that life could take things away, without warning. This was the beginning of my descent. This was the first moment I encountered the dark river that I would one day be swept into. When I found heroin, the river was waiting.

Chapter 4

Becoming Someone Else

I was torn between morbid curiosity and a repulsion of death. My body was screaming, my nervous system was on high alert, and I was overcome with fear, but I wouldn't allow myself to feel it. Instead, I repressed it. I didn't yet know how to pay attention to my inner voice or if I had the courage to follow it once the world began teaching me how to silence it. I knew now that being human felt both fragile and heavy. I needed to accept this. How was I going to find authenticity when accepting meant changing myself?

In first grade, hockey cards felt like treasure. I remember holding a rare card during recess, turning it over in my hands as if it were a prize. A boy came up and asked if he could borrow it. Other kids warned me not to hand it over. "He won't give it back," they said. I remember the split-second decision. I wanted to believe him. I wanted to show others that he could be trustworthy. More than anything, I wanted to belong. So I ignored the voice in my gut and gave it to him. I never saw the card again.

It wasn't the loss that stayed with me. It was the feeling that followed. The heat in my face. The chorus of, "We told you." The sudden understanding that my instinct had been right, and that I had overridden it to gain approval. Something small but irreversible shifted that day. I learned that if I wanted to be accepted, I might have to ignore my gut in order to belong. It was a series of little moments that created a larger redefinition of who I felt I needed to be to belong.

The emotion underneath was grief. Not dramatic grief, but the subtle kind. The kind that comes when a child realizes the world does not operate on the moral rules he hoped it would. I began to guard myself more carefully after that. I watched interactions before stepping into them. I measured tone. I studied the dynamics of power. I didn't stop wanting connection, but I began protecting myself from the cost of it.

I often describe my childhood as loving and intellectually rich, and that is true. My family was strong in many ways. But socialization outside the home felt like entering a foreign system without a manual. The playground had hierarchies. There were unspoken rules about dominance, humor, and status. I felt visible in my mistakes and invisible in my intentions. Scrutinized but not understood. That tension between wanting to belong and feeling fundamentally out of place became one of the silent pressures shaping me long before I ever touched a substance.

Boys learn quickly what earns safety and what earns ridicule. Sensitivity is tested. Trust is negotiated. By adolescence, the currency shifts from trading cards to alcohol. The environment changes from recess to parties. The motivation shifts from simple approval to social power. For those of us who learned early to override our intuition in order to fit in, substances can later feel like relief. They dull the hyper-vigilance. They simulate belonging without requiring the vulnerability we once paid for.

In response to the hockey card betrayal, I did not become tougher. I became quieter, guarded in a way that didn't draw attention. I began managing how others saw me, not by performing dominance, but by shrinking just enough to avoid becoming a target. I spoke less. I revealed less.

It's a strange experience for a child, to feel both overly visible and unseen at the same time. My missteps were public, but my interior world was hidden. No one could see how much calculation was happening beneath the surface. I wasn't trying to deceive anyone. I was trying to survive socially without losing myself more.

The cost of that strategy is subtle. When we repeatedly override our instincts to maintain connection, we slowly begin disconnecting from ourselves. The body still speaks, tightness in the chest, a flicker of intuition, but we learn not to listen. Belonging becomes something valued rather than what is experienced internally. From the outside, that looked like a well-adjusted, thoughtful child. From the inside, it felt like living behind a pane of glass.

I've come to understand that many young boys navigate this terrain in silence. There are unspoken lessons about strength, humor, hierarchy, and safety. Sensitivity can be misread as weakness. Trust can be tested publicly. When the pressure to belong outweighs the security of being oneself, adaptation begins.

By adolescence, the methods change, but the pattern remains. Partying, bravado, sarcasm, detachment, these are not random behaviors. They are tools for navigating social risk. For someone who learns early to override his gut in order to fit in, substances don't initially feel destructive. They feel regulating. They lower the stakes of social exposure. They offer connection without requiring raw vulnerability.

If I could stand beside that first-grade version of myself, the one watching his hockey card disappear into someone else's pocket, I wouldn't tell him to be tougher. I wouldn't tell him to fight back. I would tell him this: "Trust your intuition despite the social pressures. Don't become someone else to survive."

I didn't know then that abandoning myself in small social moments would compound over time. The need for belonging began to replace authenticity. Shrinking would slowly turn into fragmentation. The distance between who I was and who I presented would widen until I no longer knew which version was real.

PART II

DESCENT

Chapter 5

First Undoing

My first brush with death cracked something open in me, and my first heartbreak showed me how easily my soul could slip through that crack. I was twelve when I met her, thirteen when I started to love her, and fourteen when I realized love could hurt in ways far deeper than I was prepared for.

Even though we both attended the same middle school, I didn't know her. Summertime often involved socializing with friends at the public pool. It was there that I met her. Our relationship developed quickly and lasted on and off for two years. We spent the majority of our time at her house, hanging out while her parents were there. Our relationship was intense; we spent every day after school together but rarely crossed paths in school.

She was a year older, which felt like a lifetime at that age. She moved with a confidence I didn't yet have, spoke like the world belonged to her, and looked at me like I was special, before I ever believed that about myself. I didn't know it then, but she would become the blueprint for every emotional wound that followed.

One afternoon I walked into her bedroom and froze. My name, RORY, was written in black Sharpie across her walls. Hundreds of times, ceiling to floor, everywhere I looked, there I was. At that age, I didn't know how to interpret devotion. All I felt was shock, then embarrassment, then a sense of awe. No one had ever cared for me like that. No one had ever reflected me back to myself with such intensity.

Love came easily at that age, without expectations, without fear, without the wounds that would come later. We were kids, but our feelings weren't small. They were pure in a way only youth allows. But purity never lasts. Not in life. Not in love.

One day, I introduced her to my close friend. The following day, she broke up with me to date him. No explanation. No argument. No warning. Just a clean, crushing severance. It was the first time I felt the ground fall out from under me without anyone there to catch me. My world didn't implode, it hollowed. Everything felt muted, drained of color, flattened. It wasn't heartbreak the way adults described it. There were no dramatic tears, no diary entries, no catharsis. I felt like someone had reached inside me and unplugged something essential. I was disoriented, confused, and crushed.

Over the following year, we would get back together, and she would break up with me and return to me in cycles, weekly, sometimes twice a week. Each reunion: boundless joy. Each breakup: great despair. I learned early what it meant to love someone whose affection was unstable, unpredictable, and conditional. It taught me to brace myself, to anticipate loss before it came. It taught me not to trust the ground beneath my feet. It taught me that love could vanish, and when something vanishes early in life, you spend years trying to find something that feels like it can't be taken away.

By the time I entered high school, I was exhausted, emotionally threadbare in ways I wouldn't untangle until adulthood. So I ended it, over voicemail. Not out of cruelty, but out of necessity. It was the only power I had left. I didn't speak to her again for more than four years. And here's the truth I didn't understand then: we do not recover from early heartbreak, we carry it forward. It becomes part of the architecture of our choices. It becomes the ghost that whispers, "You can be left."

For six months after our final breakup, I genuinely believed I would never love anyone again. Days turned gray, months passed without variance. The world didn't hurt, it just felt empty. Emptiness has its own gravity. Its own quiet pull toward whatever fills it quickly. It wasn't dramatic sadness, just a dull, persistent sense that the world was moving on without me. Days repeating themselves with no clear reason to care whether they ended or began again. For a long time, that was how life felt to me. I wasn't actively unhappy, I just wasn't fully living. I watched myself move through routines, school, friendships, conversations, and substances with the sense that something essential was missing, I felt numb to it all.

Everything looked normal from the outside. Inside, it felt slightly off, like a room where the furniture had been rearranged. The feeling didn't announce itself as despair. It was subtler than that, a crevassing distance growing between who I was and who I believed I needed to be. When that distance grows large enough, something eventually fills the gap. Addiction doesn't always begin with a substance; sometimes it begins with a person. Sometimes it begins with the first door that closes your heart, and the cold that follows. I didn't know it then, but this was the beginning of the space inside me that heroin would one day occupy.

Chapter 6

The Catalyst

I use the phrase best friend to describe Hunter. I do not use that term lightly. He was my closest ally outside of my own family, and I believed he might one day change the world in ways I could only imagine.

My first girlfriend cracked my sense of safety in love. Hunter cracked my sense of safety in life itself. He wasn't just my best friend. He was the kind of person whose presence shifted the energy of every room he walked into. He carried a brightness that didn't feel performative, it felt ancestral. Like some people are simply born with more light than the rest of us. Even now, I struggle to find a comparison that doesn't feel like an exaggeration.

The truth is simple: Hunter was extraordinary. He was gracious. He was athletic. He was brilliant in an effortless way that felt unfair when I was trying desperately to understand my own place in the world. People were drawn to him, many followed him. Hunter had a complicated relationship with the way people gravitated toward him. A sort of reluctance towards them. A couple of our friends began dressing like him, speaking with the same cadence, even trying to mirror his style and confidence. To me, it seemed like a kind of admiration. I thought it was impressive that someone our age could inspire that much imitation. Hunter saw it differently. He didn't like the feeling of being copied, and more than once, I remember him getting irritated about it. This bothered him in a way I couldn't comprehend at the time. Still, despite those moments of tension, we were all close. We spent our time together the way teenage friends do: laughing, arguing, pushing against each other while somehow remaining part of the same circle. He shaped my path in ways neither of us understood at the time. If I had the gift of sensitivity, Hunter had the gift of attraction, a kind of gravity that people felt before they understood.

When we were thirteen, I heard that he had smoked weed. A few weeks later, I wanted to smoke also. I wanted to be closer to whatever pull he carried, whatever glow seemed to follow him. A year or two later, he was the one who introduced me to opiates, pills, not heroin. I realize this could be interpreted as cannabis being a gateway drug, which did not feel like the case for me. The lack of honest drug education I received was more problematic then any particular substance. When he and a few friends started experimenting with opiates, naturally, I joined them. One of our close friends obtained an entire bottle of Vicodin after getting his wisdom teeth pulled. None of us had the language for addiction yet. I wasn't thinking about dangers or ruining my life. We were teenagers looking for intensity, belonging, identity, and escape. The same things half the world searches for but with much higher costs. Between ages 15-18, I infrequently dabbled with opiates, but Hunter moved from using pills to using heroin.

Then he was gone: April 24, 2010.

I was barely eighteen when he died by suicide. I was on the other side of the country with my high school girlfriend. We were sitting in Golden Gate Park when her phone rang. She answered and listened; then let out an inhuman shriek. She cried louder than anyone I had ever heard. Meanwhile, the park kept moving around us, people playing music on metal surfaces, drums, dogs running, strangers laughing, as if nothing devastating had just happened. She hung up and told me, plainly: "Hunter's dead." My reaction startled even me. I felt . . . nothing. No collapse. No tears. No immediate grief. Just a stunned, dissociated blankness, like my mind refused to process the information.

Shock has its own intelligence. It protected me until I was safe enough to fall apart. However, I did not fall apart, not then. Not when I flew back to Vermont. Not when people hugged me and said they were sorry. I didn't even believe he was dead; some part of me simply refused to accept it. As the days passed, my numbness turned to guilt.

A missed call.

The day he died, I texted him from San Francisco. I left my phone in my hostel room. Later that night, when I returned to the room, I saw that he tried to call me. I missed the call. It was late, and I figured I'd call him the following day.

The message I sent him earlier that day, before the missed call, had come from a memory, an intuitive hit that had surfaced out of nowhere.

One night, years earlier, Hunter was invited to spend the night at my house. That day was the first time we ever ingested LSD. We were still kids. It was my first psychedelic experience, and somewhere in the middle of it, another friend of ours showed up drunk to my house. I had told him repeatedly he was not welcome. I remember asking my dad over and over again if he could stay the night, and my dad finally saying, *"No, he can't spend the night. Only Hunter can sleep over. This is the fourth time you've asked me. What's going on with you tonight?"*

Meanwhile, I was trying to hold myself together through my first acid trip while reality itself felt slightly unfastened. Eventually, my dad realized the friend came to our house anyway, and both he and Hunter had to leave. That night, they slept outside on the wooden swing in the backyard with nothing but a thin bedsheet. It happened on the first night with frost that fall. My parents didn't know.

For some reason, that moment stayed with me. And years later, that morning in San Francisco, I texted Hunter out of nowhere and apologized for that night. I told him I was sorry for how it had played out, for putting him in that position, and that our friend had shown up uninvited. What I didn't know until later was that Hunter was with the same friend when I sent that text.

That night, Hunter shot himself in the head.

I will never know why he reached out. Connection, comfort, goodbye, a question, a warning, a last grasp for a friend? I will never know. Some wounds deepen precisely because their answers remain unknown.

That missed call became a splinter in my mind, not the kind you can remove, but one that that becomes part of who you are. He would forever stay fragmented within me. His death didn't push me into addiction, but it left a hollowness inside me, and addiction thrives in the hollows. There are wounds that entice oblivion. There are losses in which numbness feels safer than feeling, grieving that begs for mercy. His death was the moment life proved it could take something irreplaceable, without warning, and without explanation.

That realization was more dangerous to me than any drug. The night the universe coalesced on my ceiling, I learned the world is infinite. The day my first girlfriend left me, I learned the heart is fragile. The day Hunter died, I learned that people can choose to disappear and never come back. All of these truths formed an abyss, a downward pull, a hollow in my soul that I didn't yet know how to defend. And into that hollow, addiction would eventually begin to grow. When relief finally appeared, I didn't question its intention.

In the weeks after he died, something else began to happen that I couldn't fully make sense of at the time. When he was alive, he would get irritated when people tried to copy him. His way of speaking, the way he moved through the world, even the way he dressed. He had a distinct presence, and he didn't like seeing it imitated.

After he was gone, that same presence began to spread. I started to notice more people dressing like him. White tank tops, skinny jeans, a shoelace threaded through the belt loops to hold them just above their thighs, the exact way he wore them. It wasn't one or two people. It was many. His favorite color, purple, was suddenly everywhere. Classmates' Facebook profile pictures changed, posts about Hunter appeared, and then something stranger. People speaking about him as if they had known him deeply. As if they had been close friends. Some of them had barely known him at all.

I don't say that with judgment. I think people were trying to hold onto something they felt slipping away. When someone like that disappears, what remains isn't just memory, it's an impression. And people try, in their own way, to impress upon that memory, to reshape it, and claim it. Watching it happen, I couldn't shake the feeling that the person I knew was being replaced by a version of him that didn't quite belong to him anymore. I never once tried to dress like him or speak like him. Something in me resisted that instinct. But I was watching something just as powerful unfold, identity dissolving and reforming in real time.

Chapter 7

The Crash

It was August 2010, and Hunter's death was four months earlier. That weighed on me even if I didn't acknowledge it then. The night of the accident, I started drinking early, and I was drunk before I arrived at the party. When I got there, I picked up the pace. I was already loud, unsteady, and convinced I was fine. The party was at a friend's house, but he wasn't there. His sister was hosting.

I remember arriving, and I immediately began to command the space. I was loud and socialized with everyone there, even the people I didn't know. That was my move back then: drinking heavily, controlling the atmosphere through volume and a large presence, and confidence through excess. The alcohol gave me a false sense of self-assurance, and Hunter's death led to a fatalistic approach to everything. This was in sharp contrast to who I was growing up.

At the party, I started drinking spiced rum straight from the bottle. I kissed the girl hosting the party more than once. I stayed for hours, or at least I think I did. The truth is, I don't remember much of it: just flashes, laughter, noise, motion.

I was unraveling. Hunter's suicide had broken something in me that I didn't have language or tools for and grief didn't look like sadness; it looked like recklessness . . . like urgency . . . like not wanting to be alone with myself for even a moment. Drinking was a form of escape. Since Vermont has one of the highest rates of underage drinking in the country, many parents were resigned to it. I could tell my parents worried about me, but they hoped I'd figure it out on my own. The reality is there wasn't much they could do. Drinking and drugs also weren't a big problem for me until after Hunter's death. This level of needing to escape was new to me.

At some point, I decided I needed to leave. I wanted to drive home. I wouldn't let anyone talk me out of it. A friend got into the passenger seat. That's the part that makes my chest still clench. I wasn't just endangering myself; I was taking someone else with me.

I made it less than a quarter mile down the dirt road. The car hit a tree and everything stopped all at once. My '98 Volkswagen Jetta was totaled. I don't remember any of it, but was told later that I broke my spine, my C6 vertebrae. The sound of the crash carried back to the house, and people came running. Someone pulled me from the car. Someone I barely knew called 911. The passenger was thankfully unharmed.

I woke up days later in the hospital. I do remember the Morphine. I remember the IV drip, the way it softened everything. Not just the pain in my neck, but the weight I'd been carrying without realizing it. There was a warmth to it, a sense that something had finally intervened. The most addictive feeling in the world - *relief.*

The surgery came and went. The prescriptions followed. The doctor gave me prescriptions for Dilaudid, many more than I needed. That isn't hindsight, that was clear even then. My mother knew it immediately. She was furious. She went into the neurosurgeon's office with me and told him he was overprescribing. She told him the dosage wasn't appropriate and that it wasn't safe.

My mother wasn't speaking as a panicked parent. She was speaking as a medical professional. A nurse practitioner who understood exactly what she was seeing. Unfortunately, he didn't listen. That moment changed something in her permanently. The absurdity of the situation wasn't lost on any of us. My mother, a psychiatric nurse, and my father, a psychiatrist, both believed in responsible and ethical medical care. Here was a doctor who they trusted, irresponsibly doling out a substance that would dramatically reorder my life.

Although I had used opiate pills before the accident, it was recreationally, and only with friends, not habitually. After the accident, that all changed. Prescription . . . prescription . . . habit . . . addiction. The hydromorphone didn't just manage pain; it taught my nervous system a new solution. Relief arrived chemically and reliably. What followed didn't look like a sudden fall. It looked like normalization, a gradual dependence that didn't announce itself as danger. Looking back, the accident wasn't just physical trauma. It was an intersection where grief, injury, access, and neglect converged. A place where relief was offered faster than understanding.

Chapter 8

Heroin

The False Sun

By December of 2010, the prescriptions had run out and heroin entered my life for the first time. A lot of my high school friends had moved on to college, and I was still recovering from spinal surgery. Heroin didn't feel like darkness; it felt like warmth, like a sun rising in a sky that had been cold for a long time. I didn't realize then that it was a false sun, one that would eventually eclipse everything else.

People talk about addiction as if it begins with a bad choice, a weak moment, or a moral slip. That's not how it works. Addiction doesn't start with the drug; addiction starts with a reason, a wound, a longing, a whisper that grows too loud to ignore.

Heroin wasn't a substance to me in the beginning. It was an answer. Before I ever touched a needle, something in me had already been looking for relief. Heroin didn't walk into a healthy and whole life. It walked into the fragmented parts of my being and made itself a home.

The first time I injected heroin, it wasn't dramatic. There was no cinematic fall, no conspicuous moment of surrender, and no awareness of the dependence that would ensue. I was with friends, with the effortless momentum of adolescence pulling us forward. Hunter had tried it, and even though he just died, I trusted him. I also needed a different escape. In a strange way, heroin became the hinge that kept our fragile circle from breaking apart after his death. It was the only language of grief we knew how to speak. I wanted to belong. I wanted to feel something that didn't hurt. When the heroin hit, it didn't feel like poison. It felt like permission. Permission to breathe without heaviness, permission to feel confident, to stop bracing for the next loss, to exist without the ache of everything inside me. People think heroin makes you numb, but the truth is more complicated. Heroin made me feel certain, stable, strong, and whole. All the confusion, the self-doubt, and the identity fragmentation went silent. It was as if someone pressed a warm hand against my chest and told me, "You can rest now."

Heroin was intoxicating in the deepest sense. It didn't just change how I felt; it changed who I thought I was. Heroin gave me an identity. For someone like me, someone who struggled to understand my own place in the world, it was the ultimate cure, not a cure for pain, a cure for uncertainty and lack of connection. Confidence came cheaply. Self-worth came instantly. The fear of loss and death evaporated. Even the danger didn't frighten me.

I was young and believed I was invincible. Somewhere in my mind, I thought, "If I use it with intention, I can't die." That's the kind of logic only a young man under the spell of delusion can create, and I believed it completely. The daily fear came much later. The fear that whispered, "You may never get off this, it will kill you, you are losing yourself." But at the start, it wasn't fear. It was relief.

Chapter 9

First Overdose

In my life, I have overdosed more times than I can remember. I stopped counting after the sixth or seventh. Each one erased the illusion that I was in control, and yet somehow, each time, despite the risk, I convinced myself it would never happen again.

In my first two years of using, I didn't yet understand what I was risking because I had never experienced an overdose before. The danger was still intangible. Methadone was still a completely foreign concept to me. In my mind, addiction still existed somewhere in the distance. I thought I was simply toying with something dangerous, not stepping into a way of life that would try to kill me.

I was twenty years old the first time I overdosed. My parents were at a conference, and I had the house to myself. Someone told me that a new batch of heroin from Chicago had just arrived in Burlington. The moment I heard that, my mind lit up like dry tinder catching a spark. The thought consumed me instantly. Getting heroin in those days always felt like a race. Everything about it carried a sense of urgency and secrecy, rushing across town, sneaking around, trying to make sure no one saw what I was doing.

I drove to Burlington, picked up the drugs, and hurried back home. By the time I had everything ready upstairs, the ritual of it all felt familiar: the spoon, the water, the flame, the careful preparation that I used to convince myself that I was in control. But as the powder dissolved, something caught my attention. The water in the spoon turned a much darker color than I was used to seeing. I noticed it. But I didn't stop. I drew the liquid into the syringe and injected only about half of it. Almost immediately, an overwhelming wave of euphoria surged through my body. But within seconds, something else followed: a heavy, disorienting incoherence that felt wrong. My thoughts blurred together. My body felt unstable, like it no longer belonged entirely to me.

I knew something was wrong. I rushed downstairs to Ryan. The moment he looked at my face, he could tell something wasn't right. I barely had the ability to form words, but I managed to tell him the truth "I used drugs. I did too much. I need help."

Ryan was naive to drug use. Neither of us had ever faced something like this before. He didn't know what to do, yet instinctively, he helped guide me to the couch and sat me down. As he tried to figure out what was happening, he repeatedly called our parents.

No one answered . . . he called again . . . and again, more than ten times.

After nearly thirty minutes, my dad picked up. Fortunately, the conference they were attending wasn't far from home. They immediately began driving back. The last thing I remember before losing consciousness was the room beginning to fade around me.

The next memory I have is of my mother's voice. In my mind, it sounded distant, like an echo moving through a long tunnel. She later told me that she was shouting my name over and over again, trying desperately to wake me up while my father called for an ambulance. I laid on the floor, Cheyne-Stokes breathing, the kind of breathing people experience at the end of their life, grasping for the last bit of air.

Inside that fading space between consciousness and darkness, it felt as though there were two directions I could go. I could let go and fall deeper into the abyss that was pulling me downward. It was enticing. In that moment, it honestly would've been easier to let go. Once I connected to my mothers voice I was called back to consciousness. Truly, there was never really a choice to make.

I followed her voice. In an instant, I was thrown back into my body. When my eyes opened, my parents were kneeling beside me, and paramedics were walking through the front door.

In the aftermath of that overdose, an addiction doctor told me that I should begin taking methadone. He explained that it would stabilize my life, prevent future overdoses, and stop the habitual cycle of heroin use before it had the chance to take a deeper hold. At twenty years old, that sounded like a solution. It sounded like protection, like a way to step back from the edge I had just nearly fallen over. The reality was more complicated than that.

Methadone did not end my addiction. It changed the shape of it. Methadone saves lives and at times saved mine. My use was complicated, like many addicts, and my heroin use didn't disappear after methadone. In many ways, it intensified. The overdoses didn't stop either. In the years that followed, they would continue, again and again, each one another reminder that the cycle I had stepped into was far from finished. At this point, I truly believed I had survived the worst of it. I had no idea I was only at the beginning.

I told myself the first overdose had been a warning. Something reckless, something avoidable. The doctor's prescription for methadone seemed like a safeguard, a way to keep the danger contained while I figured my life out. But addiction rarely moves in predictable patterns. The years that followed blurred together in a cycle of dependence that slowly grew out of hand. What began as a desperate attempt to control heroin became a life organized around avoiding sickness, chasing relief, and convincing myself that I still had time to change.

Over the years, that illusion had worn thin. This is what most people don't understand about overdose. Survival often doesn't lead to positive transformation. Survival from an overdose often means one thing: the cycle isn't finished yet.

Chapter 10

Cheating Death

I was twenty-five when a close friend, Calla, died from an overdose. She was a year ahead of me in high school. She was the kind of person who was friendly with everyone. She had a sweetness about her that people naturally gravitated toward. It seemed like everyone knew her, and most people liked her.

Her family had a reputation for being lively and fun, one of those families that people associated with parties, laughter, and a kind of carefree spirit. But years after we had all graduated, that image had faded. She had begun struggling with heroin.

One night she was staying at a persons house we both bought drugs from, only a few miles away from where I lived. I texted her asking if she could help me get what I needed, and she said if I drove to her she could meet me across the road. I took my dad's car and headed out. It was dark, and the road was barren. After a few minutes, I saw her walking toward the car. She climbed in and showed me what she had: heroin and cocaine. For someone like me, an IV drug user at this point, that combination felt like hitting the jackpot. I paid her and drove back home.

A couple of hours later, sometime around 1:00 a.m. in the morning, my phone buzzed. It was Calla. She texted saying she wasn't feeling well and asked if I could come pick her up. I told her I didn't have access to a car anymore. I told her that if she could get a ride to my place, she could stay the night. She never responded. I assumed she was okay. Earlier that night, Calla told me there were other people staying at the house with her, so I figured someone else must be around.

The next morning, I was out of drugs and driving to Burlington for my daily dose of methadone. At the clinic, I ran into an acquaintance, someone I used drugs with before but would not consider a friend. He said, "Hey, did you hear about that girl who overdosed last night?" My stomach tightened. "No," I said. "Who?" He answered, "A girl named Calla."

For a moment, everything inside me went still. Then I asked the only thing my mind could grasp onto. "Is she okay?" People overdose all the time, I thought. Most of them survive. He said he didn't know. A few hours later, when I got back home, I saw the confirmation on Facebook. Someone posted, she died. Her overdose didn't just shake me. It rippled through the entire community here in Vermont. For me, there was something heavier beneath the shock, a haunting awareness that just hours before she died, she had reached out to me.

For a long time afterward, that night lingered in my mind. Not as a single memory, but a series of questions that had no clear answers. I thought about the text she sent. I thought about the moment I did not go. In the world we were living in, those kinds of decisions were ordinary. People were always sick, always needing rides, always trying to get somewhere safer. Most of the time it ended with someone sleeping it off and waking up the next morning.

But not this time.

What made her death especially difficult to process was how ordinary the night had seemed. There had been no warning, no sense that anything final was about to happen. Just a short drive, a quick exchange, a text message in the middle of the night. It reverberated in me how thin the line had become between life and death in the world I was living in. For people like us, survival often came down to chance, who used first, who used last, whose body held on a little longer than the next.

Calla's death forced me to confront something I had been trying not to feel: that death was right around the corner. I overdosed countless times, and I'm still here. What I came to understand is that as addiction deepens, isolation follows. As isolation grows, the margin for survival narrows. It isn't always about how much someone uses, but whether anyone is there when something goes wrong. In my own life, there were moments where someone was there to pull me back, to interrupt what could have been final. Yet despite this realization, my behavior continued.

By twenty-five, I had already watched several people I cared about disappear into addiction, overdose, or prison. At the time, it still felt like a string of tragic coincidences, as if fate had simply been cruel to a few unlucky people. Somewhere deeper down, I knew the truth was much simpler and much darker. I was living with an affliction that was slowly killing me.

One year and three months after Calla's death, I heard about another girl who died. Jane lived a few towns over from where I grew up, but for a brief moment in my life, our worlds overlapped. When I was in fourth grade, I spent a year at a small Catholic school. One classroom per grade, first through eighth. For that year, we shared the same classroom. At that age, whatever I felt wasn't something I had the language for yet, but I remember liking her in an innocent way. I think she liked me too. After that year, I went back to public school, and our lives separated completely.

I only saw her twice after that. The first time was years later, after I had graduated high school. I reached out to her, and she came over one night. We sat together, watching TV, nothing remarkable on the surface. Just two people who had once known each other, reconnecting in a simple, innocent way. At that point, I didn't know she was using heroin, and I don't believe she knew I was either.

The second time was different. By then, I had heard she was using. She had just come back from Baltimore, a place where heroin was everywhere. When we met again, it was at night, and eerily reminiscent of the experience with Calla. Another quick exchange in my car, under darkness. She had a lot of drugs. More than I expected. But what stayed with me wasn't what she brought, it was how she looked. She was visibly shaken, crying as she told me her dad was in the hospital. There was something unraveling in her, something raw and immediate. When I tried to pay her, she wouldn't take the money. She just handed me the drugs and left. In that moment, it didn't feel like a transaction. It felt like something else entirely. Like she was trying to give something away that she couldn't carry anymore. She left, and I never saw her again.

About six months later, she died from an overdose. After she passed, her community felt it deeply. Her parents carried on her legacy. They started an organization, an attempt to create meaning from something that never should have happened.

I've thought about that night many times since . . . how our paths mirrored each other . . . how similar those last encounters were . . . the darkness . . . the exchange . . . the unspoken pain beneath it all. In both cases, I drove away and kept surviving. Both these deaths affected me deeply. This, however didn't stop my drug use, it only made it worse. I didn't want to face the profound feelings that surfaced with Hunter's death, the opioid deaths, the guilt of surviving while other people were dying, and the overarching grief.

The question remains - why them and not me?

Looking back, those encounters feel less like separate memories and more like reflections of the same moment, repeating itself in different forms. The same patterns, the same pain, the same unraveling happening just beneath the surface. I thought I was moving through my own story. In reality, we were all caught in the same current, drifting in and out of each other's lives, carrying the same pain in different bodies. And what I understand now is this: addiction does not take lives all at once. It sucks the life out of us slowly, until the will to live no longer remains.

For many Vermonters, who don't go off to college after high school, myself included, we can feel lost and vulnerable to addiction. Vermont's high rate of opioid use is often the result of a "perfect storm" of factors. Vermont is so remote that distractions are hard to come by. There also isn't much promise for career opportunities for young adults here given the high cost of living. This, coupled with a strong influx of out-of-state heroin dealers and a history of widespread prescription painkiller misuse, makes addiction feel inevitable for some.

Calla and Jane were the kind of people who carried light with them. They both cared deeply about others and life itself. They were full of love and complexity. The tragedy is that overdose often gets reduced to a stereotype of brokenness or failure, when in reality, these were people coping with more than any of us could see. Their deaths weren't a reflection of who they were, but rather a reflection of a crisis that can touch even the kindest of souls.

Chapter 11

The Walk

By the time I was twenty-seven, I'd been cycling through heroin for most of my adult life. The amount of drugs I was consuming had reached a level that even the people around me struggled to understand. Many of the men I used with had spent most of their lives in addiction. They had seen decades of heroin, pills, crack use, overdoses, and relapses. Yet more than once, one of them looked at me with a kind of uneasy disbelief and told me they had never seen anyone use as much heroin and crack as I was using. At the time, I barely registered what that meant. When addiction becomes the norm, scale loses its meaning. The days blur into a single objective: getting high, staying high, and repeating the cycle again and again.

One summer afternoon, I took a casual walk with a friend. We talked, no agenda, just the kind of talk that sometimes becomes a mirror held up to your life. She said, gently but firmly, "You're getting older, Rory. You need a plan to get off heroin and stay off." Normally, I would've said something like, "It's not that bad" or "I'll get off soon." That day, something changed. An intrusive flash of insight struck deep. I finally admitted to myself: "I don't think I will get off heroin. I think I'm going to die from it." I consoled myself with the thought, "at least it won't be a painful death." This didn't feel dramatic. It felt logical. It was a truth I had been orbiting for years but finally allowed myself to look at directly.

Looking back now, I see that moment clearly: a man walking the neighborhood, beard unkempt, hair unruly, scars on the inside of both elbows, finally accepting that he was no longer in control. That walk was the beginning of the end, or more accurately, the end of the beginning. Before I could transform who I was, I needed more than a realization. I needed an awakening.

PART III

AWAKENING

Chapter 12

My First Ayahuasca Experience

Three months after accepting that I may never get off heroin, I had the opportunity to take ayahuasca. At this point in my life, I only knew psychedelics in the same way I knew heroin, as an escape. I was unaware that drugs could be used to confront my pain rather than relieve it. This changed on Thanksgiving Day, 2019.

My brother Ryan came to me full of hope. He discovered something he thought could help me overcome my addiction. Ryan had been researching alternatives to conventional treatments. He found promising research with psychedelics, like psilocybin and ayahuasca, for re-patterning behavioral conditioning. He successfully brewed ayahuasca and saw benefit in his own life. He thought, *"This could help Rory."*

Ayahuasca is a psychedelic plant medicine that originated in the Amazon rainforest. It's a brew that contains the leaves of Psychotria viridis, commonly known as Chacruna, a DMT-containing plant; and the Banisteriopsis caapi vine, sometimes referred to as the vine of the soul, which contains a naturally occurring MAOI. The indigenous people of South America discovered that when taken together, it can provide a very spiritual experience.

Purging is often described as a central part of the ayahuasca experience. Many people vomit, sometimes intensely, as the body and mind release what no longer serves them. It's not typically viewed as something negative, but rather as a form of cleansing. Interestingly, in my first experience, I didn't have this reaction at all, which showed me early on that the medicine meets each person differently. My purge was more psychological than physiological.

No medical professional in the United States would have advised us to do what we did. There were no clinics available to us, no supervised programs, and no legitimate pathways for someone in my condition to explore this kind of treatment. So we made a decision that many people may question. We took the matter into our own hands.

The alternative was not safety. The alternative was continuing down the path I was already on: heroin, methadone, overdosing, and a life that was rapidly collapsing. Death was no longer a distant possibility. It was inevitable. Faced with that reality, this experience was not reckless; it was desperate. It felt like a final attempt to change my life, and it worked.

November 28, 2019, was a monumental Thanksgiving, in a way that didn't feel like a normal holiday. It felt like a threshold. I had committed to taking ayahuasca, but all morning I resisted it. I argued with myself in silence, pacing between certainty and avoidance. My ambivalence was voiced as internal doubt, "not today, later would be better," and "I'm not ready." I was ready, and I wasn't. I didn't know what to expect and was afraid to hope, I was even more afraid that it might work, and I'd have to change my life.

That tension, the push and pull between who I was and who I might become, followed me through the hours until noon, when Ryan handed me the cup. He had done the research and drank it before. I trusted him more than I trusted myself.

Ryan was sober on Thanksgiving and we planned for him to facilitate the experience and to sit with me in my old bedroom while I lay on my bed, waiting. I drank it. Nothing happened. The minutes crawled, thick and anticlimactic. An hour passed, then another. We almost gave up. At around 2:30 p.m. Ryan said he was going downstairs to help with Thanksgiving dinner. I told him that was fine and that I didn't feel anything from the dose anyway. He walked out feeling dejected. He thought he had failed me.

The door closed, and within five minutes, everything shifted. The first sensation was lightness, a subtle lift inside my chest, as if someone had untied a knot I didn't know was there. My vision sharpened. Tracers feathered the edges of movement. Colors held longer in the air. Then something else rose, not euphoria, not intoxication, but confidence.

A confidence I hadn't felt since I was 13 years old. I wasn't afraid; I was present. I sat on the bed for forty minutes, watching a video of a professional UFC fighter going through his daily routine, training, eating, and stepping into cryotherapy. My mind registered the footage differently than usual. What a luxury it is to live like this, I thought. To have a purpose that commands your body and your time.

Downstairs my older brother Brendan, a professional hockey player, was preparing for dinner. The parallels weren't lost on me. He and the UFC fighter were living their purpose, and I was lost and oft forgotten. It was time to go join my family for Thanksgiving dinner.

At the top of the staircase something made me stop. I turned to my right and saw myself in the large mirror: long hair, long curled beard, scars in the crook of my arms. The familiar voice rose immediately, "You can't go down there, just go back to your room, hide." But as that instinct surfaced, the instinct I had listened to for years, a second voice rose behind it, "You're fine. Nothing is wrong. Your family loves you. Go join them."

It wasn't gentle. It wasn't coddling. It was decisive. It felt like someone had stepped into my body and spoken for me, not taking control, but restoring it. And so, I obeyed it. I walked downstairs.

My family was seated at the table, the white cloth shimmering under the light in a way that made it look almost alive. My niece, Eevee, was born in the same house, not even 36 hours earlier. She was joining us for her first family dinner.

I sat down with no food on my plate, which for a Thanksgiving meal was unheard of, and whispered to Ryan, "I'm tripping, man." But I wasn't afraid. For the first time in years, I felt like I belonged in my own body, like I was actually in the room with the people I loved. Conversations peaked, emotions came alive. I was present! There was no euphoria, just clarity, a clarity I had been running from for almost a decade. A subtle thought formed: "This is what clean feels like." I felt cleansed and awakened, and it was divine.

People think awakening is bliss. It isn't. Awakening was the moment I saw my life without distortion, and I could no longer lie to myself about who I'd become. As the ayahuasca unfolded, I saw the decade behind me not as random chaos but as a pattern: Hunter's death at eighteen, the wounds I never faced, the years of heroin, the borrowed confidence I mistook for identity, the first overdose with Ryan calling our parents while I slipped under, and the six or seven more overdoses that followed, each one a warning I ignored. All of it was replayed not as a punishment, but as a map. After the experience, I was able to accept Hunter's death and all of these moments more completely.

Ayahuasca didn't erase the past. It illuminated it. It didn't tell me I was healed. It told me I had to stop running. It didn't grant me salvation. It handed me responsibility, and in that moment, surrounded by family, I realized something that stopped me cold: I did not want to die. That was the awakening. Not visions, not colors, not revelations. I wanted to live and for the first time in years, change felt possible.

The experience wasn't overwhelming. It didn't knock me out or send me to the floor. It simply lifted the veil. It widened my chest, spiritually, emotionally, literally, and let me stand inside myself without flinching. It showed me who I had been pretending to be, and who I might become if I stopped running. Most importantly, it showed me what silence had been costing me. What heroin had been costing me. What my absence had been costing the people who loved me.

Ayahuasca didn't heal me that day. It revealed me to myself. It was the first moment in a decade where I saw a path forward. One that required work, discipline, and sacrifice, yes, but a path that existed. That alone changed everything, because until that day, I genuinely believed I would die addicted.

And somehow, sitting at that table with a glowing white cloth and the people who made me, I realized who I could become.

Chapter 13

Methadone Detox

The cravings that ruled my life for years were suddenly gone. I stopped using heroin overnight after the ayahuasca, not through willpower or discipline, but because something deeper had changed in the way I saw myself. I took a piece of paper and wrote down two goals. First was, "Get off methadone!" Followed by the second, "Change addiction therapy."

I set out to accomplish the first goal, to get off methadone. Methadone is meant to stabilize lives. For many people, it does exactly that. It keeps some people away from heroin, reduces overdoses, and gives them the space to rebuild their lives. But that wasn't my experience. When I started on methadone at age twenty, I never imagined I would still be trapped in that world seven years later. I didn't want to be someone who used opiates for the rest of his life. Yet somehow, the years kept passing and the cycle continued. Methadone didn't remove heroin from my life; it existed alongside it. Instead of freeing me from opiates, it anchored me deeper to them. That was why the conviction to get off methadone felt so urgent after ayahuasca. It wasn't simply about stopping one medication. It was about refusing to live a life that remained dependent on opiates. Deep down, I knew that as long as that dependency remained, heroin would never be far behind.

Even as I felt the beginning of a new direction opening in my life, I knew I was still tethered to the methadone. Every morning I woke up knowing that my body was still dependent on it. The more honest I became with myself, the clearer one conviction grew: if I wanted to reclaim my life, I had to get off methadone.

For the first time in years, I felt a responsibility to my life that was stronger than the fear of withdrawal. I was going to finish what had started that night with ayahuasca. Taking responsibility always sounds noble in theory. In practice, it is inconvenient, terrifying, and deeply unglamorous. For me, responsibility crystallized in a medical office, a place I had visited hundreds of times, but never as the man I was becoming. I told my Ryan I wanted him to come with me to my appointment with the methadone doctor.

He agreed, though I later learned he didn't understand why I asked. He thought I might be manic, riding the afterglow of the ayahuasca trip. He wasn't wrong to wonder. I had been hypomanic before, but this wasn't mania. This was conviction.

When I told Ryan: "I'm getting off methadone," he heard the confidence and questioned the stability. Yet he also heard something deeper, a seriousness that hadn't been there in years. It had only been two weeks since my ayahuasca experience when I scheduled an appointment with the methadone doctor. In the seven years I had been on methadone, I had only met with him one other time. Most of my treatment consisted of standing in line, drinking my dose, and leaving. The system was designed to maintain stability, not necessarily to ask questions about where you wanted your life to go.

This appointment was different. I had already made up my mind. Ryan came with me to the clinic that morning. The waiting room looked the way it always did, a steady stream of people coming and going, each there for the same daily routine. I was one of them. At times I even felt a strange sense of relief sitting there. As long as I had my dose, everything felt manageable and life could remain simple. While we waited, I looked around the room and saw people I recognized from years of standing in the same line. Most of them weren't trying to escape the system. Methadone gave them stability. In many cases it kept people alive. I understood that. It kept me alive too.

On this day, I also began noticing something else. A young man sat across the room with his mother beside him. He couldn't have been more than twenty. The look on his face struck me, not the look of someone chasing a high, but someone already resigned to a life managed by medication. I wondered how many years stretched out ahead of him, dosing at the same window every morning. I didn't see a junkie that wanted to be there. I saw a victim of a system that gave him no alternative than to "maintain" his disease on socially sanctioned numbing agents. He wanted treatment, but instead he got a less dangerous version of the same coping mechanism that he invented with heroin.

In that moment, the absurdity of it all became impossible to ignore. The pharmaceutical companies had flooded communities with opiates for decades, and the solution they arrived at was another prescription opiate, one that was deemed more socially acceptable, and people were expected to take it every day, indefinitely. For some people, that system worked. For me, it never truly had.

When the nurse called my name, Ryan and I walked toward the hallway. She told Ryan he would have to stay in the waiting room. "I want my brother to come in with me," I said. She hesitated and told me there wasn't room. "I'm not going in without him," I stated. After a moment, she left to ask the doctor. A few minutes later, the doctor himself appeared. He looked impatient. "Rory, come into my office. I don't have all day." I asked, "Can my brother come in?" He replied firmly "No." Feeling the need for my brother's support, I told the doctor, "I'm not coming in without him." He studied me for a moment, weighing whether the argument was worth the trouble. Finally, he sighed. "Fine. Bring him in."

We walked into his office and sat down. "I want to get off methadone," I said. He leaned back slightly and said, "I don't think that's a good idea." "I don't care," I replied, "I'm going to do it." He asked if I had a plan, and I told him I did. At the time, I was on 120 milligrams. I explained that I was going to cut my dose by 20 milligrams the next day, then reduce it another 20 milligrams the following day, and continue that cycle until I reached 20 milligrams. From there, I would reduce one milligram a day until I was off completely.

He shook his head almost immediately. "That's far too fast. With a dose as high as yours, we would normally taper someone over one or two years." I responded, "I don't have that much time to waste." He looked at me with a kind of clinical seriousness. "You understand the statistics, right? About ninety percent of people who try to get off methadone end up right back on it. Of the remaining ten percent, five percent succeed, and five percent die." He wasn't trying to scare me. From his perspective, he was stating a medical reality, but the statistics only motivated me more.

"Have you ever had a profound psychedelic experience?" I asked him. The question seemed to catch him off guard. After a moment, he nodded. "Years ago," he said. "I had a powerful peyote experience that changed my life." His response provided me the opening to tell him about the past six months of my life. Using heroin daily while still on methadone, shooting and smoking crack, living in complete chaos. Then I told him about the ayahuasca experience and how profoundly it affected me. "I haven't used heroin or crack since," I said. "But I realized something. Methadone is doing the same thing those drugs were doing. It's keeping me from facing myself. I haven't been sober in over seven years. I need to meet that person again."

He listened quietly. Finally, he said, "I appreciate your story, but my job is to keep people from dying. If you taper off methadone this quickly, you are likely to die." I nodded, showing him I understood the risk. "I came here out of respect for you and your profession," I told him. "But you can't make me take methadone. Tomorrow, I'm drinking half my dose." There was a long pause. Eventually, he realized there wasn't much he could do. He told the nurse to adjust my taper schedule the way I had requested.

Ryan and I left the clinic a few minutes later. The decision had already been made. The real test hadn't even begun yet. Leaving methadone wasn't heroic. It was agony. The afterglow of ayahuasca faded. The withdrawals tore through me physically and emotionally. The walls of repression broke open, but responsibility isn't measured by comfort. Responsibility is measured by endurance.

Getting off methadone was not enlightenment. It was not triumph. It was not the "rebirth" so many people romanticize when they talk about recovery. It was hell. Methadone is designed to prevent withdrawal, but that means when withdrawal finally comes, it arrives like a tidal wave with almost a decade's worth of momentum behind it. At first, I felt almost proud. The initial days weren't as bad as I expected. I told myself I was strong, that my spiritual awakening had hardened and insulated me. I was wrong.

When the methadone finally left my system, fully, brutally, the collapse began. It didn't hit my body first. It hit my mind. All the emotions methadone had numbed for seven years came roaring back at once. The guilt, the grief, the shame, the self-hatred, the wasted years, the lost friendships, Hunter, the missed call, the overdoses, the look on my brother's face, my parents aging while I spiraled, the man I could have been, the man I feared I would never become. The physical agony was bad, shakes, sweats, vomiting, tremors, skin-crawling torture, but the emotional collapse was worse.

For the first time in almost a decade, there was no opiate buffer. No chemical silence. No escape hatch. It was me versus myself, and I had not been in that ring for a very long time. Methadone didn't just protect me from withdrawal. It protected me from feeling anything real. When it left my body, everything I ever avoided came crashing down.

During the worst of it, I remember trying to lay still, feeling like my mind was splitting open. My body was convulsing. My emotions were excruciating. My sense of identity was stripped away, I couldn't figure out who I was. I had faced darkness before, during overdoses, during withdrawal, during panic, but this was different.

This was clarity without anesthesia, the truth without protection. I understood, fully and frighteningly, this is why people die on the way out. This is why people return to methadone or heroin. Not because they are weak, but because they are alone inside a storm no human being is meant to endure without help. I knew I couldn't return to methadone, but I also couldn't survive like this forever. The responsibility felt like drowning.

Years later, as I began to look deeper, the cycle I was caught in felt less like coincidence and more like design. I learned that between 2006 and 2012, the vast majority of opioid pills in the United States were manufactured and distributed by just a handful of companies. Names like Mallinckrodt, Endo, Teva, and others that would later face fines, lawsuits, and public scrutiny. One line in particular stopped me in my tracks: *"In those years, SpecGx (Mallinckrodt subsidiary) supplied 28.9 billion oxycodone pills. That equals more than 80 for every person in the United States, and over 2 billion pills in Florida alone."* It's hard to fully grasp numbers like that. Entire communities weren't just affected; they were saturated, and then died in masses.

Yet, when people like me became addicted, the path to recovery we were offered didn't lead outside that system; it led further into it. The same companies, or the structures they became part of, continue to play a major role in supplying opioid medications used in treatment today. Including methadone, in the form of Methadose (in which SpecGx is a leading producer). In many cases, that treatment is funded through public systems, supported, primarily, by taxpayer dollars. Teva and Mallinckrodt continue to generate significant revenue from "specialty generics," which include the very medications (methadone and buprenorphine) funded by the taxpayer-backed programs. Because 85% of settlement funds must be used for "opioid abatement," states are under pressure to rapidly scale programs, which often results in expanding existing high-volume medication-assisted treatment (MAT) clinics that rely on these manufacturers' products. Recycling the money back into the pockets of the pharmaceutical companies.

I don't say this to dismiss methadone. I know it saves lives. I know it creates stability where there was once chaos. But for me, it never felt like an exit. It felt like a continuation, like the system that helped shape my addiction was also shaping my "recovery." The same companies who created the problem are now profiting off the "solution." Somewhere deep down, I couldn't shake the feeling that true healing, something deeper, something closer to what I would later understand as soul-level repair, was still being overlooked. That there were other paths, less industrial, more human, that we weren't investing in, or even willing to fully explore.

In the months following ayahuasca, while I was near the end of the methadone taper, I knew something needed to change, not just internally, but structurally. I understood that if I didn't anchor myself to something real, the same gravity that pulled me into heroin for a decade would pull me back again.

I had a glimmer of hope, but I needed a vessel strong enough to hold it. A container, a practice that could hold me when my resolve weakened, when the fog returned, when the old world beckoned. That's when Ryan stepped in. He didn't approach me as a therapist. He didn't approach me as a rescuer. He approached me as a brother who refused to lose me, and together, with our friend Travis, we built something that changed us all, a weekly ritual in the woods.

It didn't begin with grand philosophy, perfect intention, or stable confidence. It began with discomfort. We met outside, in the wilderness, each Sunday, around a fire pit that became our anchor point. The cold didn't matter. The heat didn't matter. The rule was simple.

Show up every Sunday, no matter what.

Chapter 14

Overdose after Awakening

I believed I was closer to sobriety than ever before. In some ways, that was true. But addiction does not disappear because you have a spiritual awakening. Insight alone cannot dissolve a decade of using habits to numb my pain.

Without realizing it, I was still moving toward the lowest point of the descent. In the final weeks of the methadone detox I was on just two milligrams and we had just started our weekly Sunday ritual in the woods. I made a decision in a moment of weakness. I ordered heroin online.

This Sunday ritual wasn't like the ones that would come later, full of structure, intention, and clarity. This was early, raw, experimental, and unrefined. Three young men trying to find connection and purpose, while confronting the worst parts of their lives without flinching.

I was terrified, but I showed up, and I told the truth. Heroin was being delivered the next morning. I didn't trust myself to make the right decision. I admitted it. I said the words out loud. And in that admission, something in me loosened, like the thread holding the versions of myself together had finally snapped.

The following is a reflection that I wrote about this overdose, less than a year after it occurred.

———————————————————

I sat there bombarded and overwhelmed with fear. I was facing who and what I had become over the past decade. I had just had a spiritual awakening from an ayahuasca journey a few months earlier, and I was currently a couple of months into a methadone detox. I couldn't come to grips with the reality of it, but I knew being there with Ryan and Travis that I needed to be honest and come forth with what my plan was. Heroin was being delivered to my door the following morning.

I was terrified. I had been toying with death for most of my adult life. I didn't have an urge to seek drugs that day as I felt connected and part of something bigger with the ritual we were creating. But I knew the next day would be tough, and it was. The heroin was being delivered by mail whether I wanted it to be or not. So I told them, and we all agreed on a plan for Ryan to intercept the drugs before I could use them.

[The following morning]

Instinctively I woke up early, before Ryan did. As it arrived I was again faced with the decision to use or not. I felt alone again, outside of the ritual. I decided to do what I thought was a small amount.

In an instant I was out, like a light.

The next thing I know, I am forcefully thrown back into my body as my parents had just administered three doses of Narcan. I returned to consciousness with the most intense and awful pounding in my head, like I had never experienced in my life.

I felt as though my entire life was being forcefully taken and that my whole life had flashed in front of my eyes. It was the most painful physical experience I'd ever endured. I was in intense withdrawal from the Narcan, my body writhing in pain, compounded with excruciating fear that felt bone deep all the way to my core.

All I could manage to say was how sorry I was for everything I'd ever done that hurt my family. I couldn't handle the reality I was experiencing at that moment.

I just wanted more heroin to take the pain away.

This moment showed my family the truth they were trying not to see. This wasn't experimentation. This wasn't a phase. This was my life on the line, over and over again, inside a cycle bigger than my willpower and my conscious choices.

The ritual opened a door inside me, but my life outside it hadn't yet changed. I was still living in the same conditions. After this overdose, I made a personal decision to check myself into rehab. I entered rehab multiple times before, but never on my own volition. I needed a safe space to go, to get away from the temptation of opiates, to finish my methadone taper, and to walk out completely off methadone. I looked into my family's eyes while dying before. I did not want to put them through that ever again.

Luckily, I had the ritual to return to. I remember calling one Sunday while they were at the ritual spot, and I was detoxing off the last few milligrams of methadone in rehab. They were proud of me, I was proud they still chose to meet. This was extremely motivating for me at the time. The following Sunday, I rejoined the ritual.

I was finally off methadone.

PART IV

RISING

Chapter 15

The Ritual

For nearly two years, each of us missed only one Sunday ritual. At first, we didn't know how to do what we were trying to do. We didn't know how to open up. We didn't know how to tell the truth without minimizing it. We didn't know how to sit in silence with each other without filling it with jokes or distractions. We were three men sitting in the forest, at times unsure how to start a fire, but we kept showing up, and eventually, the fire illuminated our path.

Over time, the ritual took shape. Not only because we designed it, but because it revealed itself.

The pillars became clear -

Start: a group signaling or act that initiates the start of the ritual

Invocation: sit in silence as long as you possibly can, only speak when you feel absolutely compelled to say something

Show up: with the intention to confront something difficult, be prepared to expect an uncomfortable internal confrontation

Vulnerability: speak honestly, even when it hurts your pride

Trust: listen without judgment, without fixing, without controlling

Consistency: show up especially when you don't want to

Discomfort: lean into what scares you, that's where the truth is

Presence: no distractions

Validation without agreement: acknowledging each person's truth is real to them, even if not universal

My intention, especially early on, was simple: stay off opiates. But the ritual quickly became bigger than that. It became a training ground for becoming a man again, or maybe for the first time.

In the months leading up to the ritual, while I was deep into methadone withdrawals, the tension between Ryan and me was at an all-time high. He supported me to this point, but there was nothing more he could do for me. He encouraged me to uncover ten years of repressed emotion, yet he offered me no tools to deal with the pain, so I dealt with it the only way I knew how, projecting it outwardly and aggressively.

At times, my anger boiled into a blind rage, lashing out on everyone that I loved. I threatened my sister-in-law, in front of my niece. I pushed my dad to the ground, terrifying my sister Brianna. I yelled insults at Ryan until he started sobbing. For ten years, I felt unseen and unheard. Now that I didn't have the drugs to suppress my emotions, the anger could not be ignored. It was creating problems with my relationships. Leaving me feeling more alone and isolated. I was determined to make my voice heard and my physical presence known.

The anger, along with disconnection, were subsequent factors that resulted in the birth of the ritual with my brother. There are people you meet in life who feel like cosmic allies. But a brother, a real brother, is something older than fate. A brother is a mirror you cannot escape. Ryan and I were not always close. People assume brothers grow up in step with each other, but the truth is that we drifted apart as we grew older. Addiction created a distance that wasn't measured in miles but in day-to-day reality; we were living in separate worlds even when we were in the same house.

Ryan saw me slipping away long before I admitted it to myself. He saw the withdrawal behind my eyes, the emotional absences, the way I self-sabotaged relationships. He felt me pulling away even when part of me wanted to stay close. The other part of me wanted to distance myself further to protect him. When we were young, I saw my brother as the best of us. He was the distillation of our whole family. He was pure. I always tried to protect him from corrupting influences; the irony is that I became the primary source of corruption. Subconsciously, I was toying with the idea that he would be better off without me. In this way, death by overdose wasn't tragic; it was heroic. Just another lie an addict will tell himself to justify his actions.

The first overdose he witnessed didn't just scare him; it nearly drove an irreconcilable wedge between us. It forced him to confront his own helplessness. That moment, the one I barely remember, he will remember for the rest of his life.

And yet, he stayed. He kept showing up, not because he wasn't angry or afraid or exhausted, but because somewhere beneath the chaos, he still believed in me. In his eyes I wasn't the addict, but the brother he remembered.

What makes this brotherhood arc special is not the suffering; it is the return. When my awakening began, it was Ryan who recognized it first. He saw my potential before I saw it in myself. He saw that something in me was coming back to life, and he protected it when I faltered.

The ritual was not just my salvation; it was our reunion. Week after week, sitting in the wilderness by firelight, he saw the man I was becoming. He saw me fight for my own life. He saw me confront my past, the years of exploiting, manipulating, and hurting people. He held me accountable, and I began to accept what I had done. I was holding on to the pain, grief, and shame of my past. I wore them like a badge, so I'd never forget the hurt I caused. In reality, this only perpetuated the pain. I didn't feel deserving of forgiveness. Ryan, through his persistence, gave me permission to forgive myself. Eventually, he let himself hope again. This is the part most stories never capture. The transformation wasn't just mine; my brother transformed with me.

My return gave him permission to stop grieving someone who wasn't dead. When I relapsed, even after he thought the worst was behind me, he didn't abandon the bond. He didn't collapse back into hopelessness. He dug in deeper. He fought harder. He refused to accept a world where his brother died. My survival became part of his identity. His role in my transformation was no longer circumstantial; it was purposeful.

In the beginning, the ritual felt awkward. We stumbled through silence, we interrupted each other, we hid behind humor, and we only partially opened up. Week by week, the space deepened. Something ancient happens when men gather intentionally around a fire. Something that predates therapy and religion. It strips us down. It burns away the pretense. It reveals the parts of us that we pretend not to see.

Slowly, the ritual changed me. I learned to speak without performing. I learned to listen without defending. I learned to sit with discomfort instead of medicating it. I learned to recognize the voice inside me that wanted to run, and not obey it. I learned what responsibility actually feels like. The ritual stabilized the awakening. It translated insight into discipline, and for the first time in years, I felt connected to something bigger than my pain.

The ritual forced me to feel my pain and the pain that I caused others. Throughout the course of the ritual, we had been developing the courage to really examine the true fear of human existence, the fear of death. In the ritual structure we felt secure enough to look at death, and it did not overwhelm us. We had a container to examine and transform fear together. We wanted to confront fears of death and non-existence head-on. We believed the more fear we could endure, the stronger we would become.

The ritual was not designed to be peaceful. It pushed us toward the edges of ourselves. One night, the ritual broke open into something deeper and darker than any of us expected. My dad joined us. We smoked a joint, sat in silence, and let the fire do its work. At some point, I looked up and caught Ryan staring directly into my eyes, not just at me, but into me. His gaze didn't blink, soften, or break.

Immediately, I felt exposed, as if the armor I had worn for years had fallen away. But something inside me commanded, "Don't look away. Don't flinch. Stay."

We held that gaze for what felt like eternity. Then everything shifted. My heartbeat sped up. My mind began racing. Something inside me expanded, an overwhelming recognition that we were not separate, that the boundaries between us were illusory. It wasn't metaphor. It was experience. I was him. He was me. We were one. All of us were one. It terrified me. It's one thing to hurt myself, now I have to face the reality that by hurting myself I was hurting everyone else.

At that exact moment, the clouds above us darkened. Rain began to fall, just lightly, as if the world was trembling with us. Our other member, Travis, waited in anticipation, sensing something was happening but not knowing what. My father, the man who always knew what to do, looked uncertain.

Faces flashed in my mind: uncles, lineage, ancestry. It all felt connected. It was too much. I felt the existential dread that I had hidden deep in the corners of my subconscious at the age of four, when death first entered my life. The fear threatened to overwhelm me. It was terrible. I questioned aloud why we were doing the ritual, and we all considered stopping. We were scared of where this was going. But in the hours and days that followed, I felt lighter, like a weight had been lifted. We realized then that this was what the ritual was all about. Confronting the fear of death now, while we still have time to live, rather than on our deathbeds with a life full of regret and no time left.

The ritual provided me with a place to go, a structure to hold me, and a discipline that kept me tethered to reality. Each week I had something to look forward to. Every time we met in the woods, I had motivation to do better the following week. Every decision I made between meetings carried more responsibility because I knew I'd have to explain myself to my two best friends on Sunday. Their disappointment or their joy would be shared amongst us all. The ritual did not erase my darkness. It taught me how to face it without collapsing. It made me accountable. It made me honest. It made me human again. The ayahuasca showed me who I could be. The ritual taught me how to become him.

We used the word ritual because it described the function of what we were doing more accurately than any other word. Every Sunday, regardless of weather or mood, we showed up at the same place, with the same underlying intentions: to explore our inner lives, to keep one another accountable, and to express ourselves honestly and vulnerably. The structure mattered. The repetition mattered. Moving into the woods, connecting with nature, sitting in a simple geometry, marking the beginning with a shared action, and entering silence before speaking, all created the boundary between ordinary life and deliberate reflection. The boundary changed how we listened, how we spoke, and how responsible we felt to one another. There was nothing mystical about it. It was a way of slowing the mind, regulating emotion, and making space for truth to surface.

At the beginning of many of those Sundays, we shared a cannabis joint. It was the sacrament that opened the door to what a ritual could be, but as the ritual began to grow in connection and intention, the less we needed to rely on it to open that door. I had only ever been taught that drugs were bad. Ryan recognized before any of us that drugs weren't inherently good or bad; instead, their effect depended on intention. Up until this point, I knew what sacred meant but never what it felt like. In a way, the ritual was an experiment. We were testing a theory to see if we could use a substance to produce positive life changes. I doubted it. I knew too well how easily lines blur, and I remained attentive to whether the practice sharpened or softened my accountability.

An addict using a drug to help treat his addiction, especially in a non-medical context, sounds perverse to many people. They ask reasonable questions: Why this method? Why not another? Couldn't the same insights have come from something more traditional? I already spent years learning how easily relief could masquerade as healing. The ritual was never about escape, transcendence, or feeling better for a few hours. Its value wasn't in the smoke, the setting, or the symbolism; it was in what followed. The measure was always whether the practice increased honesty, accountability, and responsibility in the days that came after. Theory asks what ought to work. Lived experience answers with what actually did.

By the second summer, the ritual had softened. Not in commitment, just in tone. The emergencies were gone. The fear was gone. We had all taken a step back from the edge we were living on. One Sunday, after the fire was lit and the sun dipped behind the hill, something unusual happened. We couldn't stop laughing, not because anything was funny, not because we were avoiding something heavy, but because for the first time in years, we were light.

I was clean and sober for twelve months.

My body wasn't fighting itself. My brain wasn't clawing for opiates. There was space in me again, space enough for joy to echo. Ryan told a story about our childhood. Travis mispronounced a word and kept doubling down on it. I made fun of myself, which I hadn't been able to do in a decade. We just lost it, with the kind of laughter that leaves your face aching and your ribs sore. Halfway through the ritual, I realized I can feel joy. I can be. I can sit with myself. I can hold space with others. No dread waiting around the corner. No craving pretending to be destiny. Just presence. Ryan looked at me, wiped his eyes, and said, "You're back, Rors, not coming back, not trying to come back, back!" It was a night that made normalcy feel sacred. Maybe that's what healing actually looks like, not one grand moment, but the return of things you thought you'd lost forever. That night didn't feel holy. It felt human, and that was holy in its own way.

Months after getting off methadone, in early 2020, we were so inspired by the ritual that we started a podcast. It didn't feel like a project. It felt like a necessity. It was born out of the ritual because we wanted to continue the work we were doing on Sundays and connect more frequently. The primary goal was for Ryan and me to talk with one another authentically and vulnerably. We were using the podcast to track the commitments that came alive in the ritual and integrate them into our daily lives. There was also a desire to inspire others to start their own ritual, and examine their own sense of commitment and connection.

To our surprise, it resonated, and people listened. We were featured in two newspapers. It felt affirming, like evidence that something real was happening. We kept trying to define what we were doing. It was not therapy. The closest word we could find was "flow," the state athletes describe when effort disappears and action feels guided by something larger than thought. Even that felt incomplete. What changed was simple. Time slowed. Defensiveness eased. No one was performing. No one was trying to win. For the first time in years, connection was enough.

Chapter 16

California Nightmare

I was off of methadone and opiates for over a year. I had achieved my first goal of getting off methadone, and I was ready to attempt the second goal of changing the way our society treats addiction, or so I thought.

I went to Huntington Beach, California for an interview for our podcast. A woman online had posted about her ayahuasca experience and how it helped her overcome addiction. I wanted to interview people like her for the podcast, to gather proof that transformation was possible, that what happened to me on that Thanksgiving Day in 2019 wasn't a fluke, but the beginning of something bigger. I planned to be gone for six days, so I'd be back just in time for the next ritual, but California nearly destroyed my life. I walked straight into a waking nightmare.

The first misstep was that I knew no one in this part of California. Upon arriving, she picked me up, we went to a bar for a few hours, and then she left. I stayed watching a sports game, ironic, since nothing mattered less to me at that moment than sports. A man sat down next to me and struck up a conversation. He was charismatic, wealthy, and effortless. He owned a boat. He told me he pulled up to clubs off the coast and people watched him arrive like a movie character making an entrance. I admired him instantly, not because of the boat, but because he looked like someone who had escaped the modern-day pressures of the world.

He had no idea who I was or what past I was carrying, so when he welcomed me under his wing, I didn't hesitate.

The first night, alone in my hotel room, I searched online for sex workers, something I'd never done before in my life. I wasn't craving sex; I was craving escape and affirmation, a feeling that heroin had provided me, something to distract me from the growing sense that I'd made a mistake coming alone. I contacted one woman, realized the price was too high, and politely declined. Her reply changed everything.

It wasn't her. It was a man. He claimed cartel affiliation. He demanded payment. Somehow, he found my home address through WhatsApp. He threatened me and my family. Then came the photos. Detached heads and headless bodies, the kind of images no one forgets. My nervous system lit up like a bomb. Every instinct screamed, "I am in danger, I am alone, I have no allies, I have no protection." I didn't want to alert him and expose my fear by responding. So I froze. That freeze began to rot into paranoia, spiraling downward.

When the messages didn't stop, I reached out to the man I met at the hotel bar. He helped me obtain the only anesthesia I understood: drugs. Cocaine first. Then more cocaine, then alcohol, then weed.

Then meth for the first time in my life. From here, things got a lot worse. I didn't know where the line was anymore, and I crossed every one of them. The man from the hotel bar felt like a friend, but he wasn't a friend, and he encouraged all the things that I had been avoiding. He didn't know who he was entertaining. To him, I was an interesting out-of-towner. To me, he was a lifeline with frayed edges, and access to any drug we wanted; except he wouldn't do heroin, and so I didn't either. To the drugs, I was prey. This continued for days.

In California, the structure of the ritual that had stabilized me was absent, yet the fear remained. I had been conditioning myself to open up to fear in the ritual. When I smoked meth, all the fear flooded in without any filters. The drugs were too intense; they blasted open the fear of death, and it overwhelmed and consumed me. Paranoid delusions were the only way to cope, and everything became a threat to my life. The drugs and paranoia consumed my existence. I lost track of time and abandoned any commitment to return to Vermont after only six days.

On the tenth evening, after days of escalating use, I became absolutely certain someone was outside my room waiting to kill me. I heard hallway noises that weren't there. I saw shadows move without moving. The cartel messages played on a loop in my mind. Finally, I dialed 911, but by the time the paramedics entered my room, I wasn't sure if they were real or part of the threat.

When they strapped me to the gurney, I didn't feel safer; I felt captured. As the ambulance rolled, I was convinced the paramedic beside me was the man who'd been threatening me. I thought he was going to shoot me in the back of the head while I lay there propped up on the gurney. He was saving my life, but I was living a different reality.

I remember the emergency room only in flashes: hallucinations, grandiosity, terror. Every time they closed the curtain to my room, the metal rings scraping across the rod sounded like an AR-15 firing. I braced for bullets that never came. I couldn't sleep. I thought that if I closed my eyes, that's when I'd be killed, so I didn't allow myself to close them for longer than a blink. As the sleep deprivation increased, the delusions followed. At some point, I saw spirits, two figures on either side of my face. I couldn't look directly at them, but from the corners of my eyes I could see their outlines, their ancient, indifferent gazes. Time broke apart; minutes became hours, hours became days. I was there for 72 hours, but it felt like weeks.

The staff eventually concluded that I wasn't safe to be released on my own. They transferred me to a psychiatric facility, locked, sterile, and absolute. I believed I had crossed some invisible threshold that separated "normal people" from the forgotten ones, the ones society locks away because they don't know how to fight for themselves. I didn't belong there either, not in the way they thought. When the staff realized I wasn't violent, manic, or delusional outside the drug-induced terror, they reconsidered. My psychiatrist father spoke with them, and they agreed to release me under strict conditions. Go straight to the airport, fly home, no detours, no wandering, no stops. So I tried. I really did. But I missed three connecting flights in three different cities. Not because I didn't want to go home, but because I was still unmoored from reality and still terrified of other people.

Finally, an airline employee in Philadelphia helped me board a flight to Charlotte, where my brother Brendan and sister Brianna lived. When I stepped off the plane and saw them, something inside me loosened for the first time in weeks. They didn't say anything profound. Their presence was enough, but I still had one more flight to take to Boston. Ryan picked me up and drove me back home to Vermont. When I arrived home, I was safe; but I didn't feel safe, not even close.

The following Sunday, I returned to the ritual. Travis and Ryan took one look at me and saw how deeply my faith and sense of reality itself had been shaken. They were angry, not just with me, but at what I'd endured, at how close they had come to losing me again, at the world for being what it is, and at the drugs for nearly succeeding.

Beneath their anger was something else, determination to return to a sense of stability within the ritual. California was the bottom, the underworld, the descent no one walks out of unchanged. And in that dark place, something primal spoke in my ear: "Enough!" Not because the suffering was over, but because the suffering had taught me what it needed to. I went to California to hear a woman's story of hope from ayahuasca, and I returned with my own story of despair.

When I came back from California, I didn't fall straight back into using. The three of us continued doing the ritual, but it didn't have the same effect. For a time, I was still holding onto something, some thread of clarity, some sense that what I had experienced was something I could make meaning from. But after a few months, I started using opiates again, occasionally, not with the same frequency as in the past.

At this time, a documentary filmmaker began taking interest in what we were doing. He had listened to our podcast. He also saw my story in a local newspaper about getting off methadone and stepping away from heroin. He saw this as something that could be of interest to others and maybe even replicated.

I was unable to be honest with others that I was using again. Still traumatized from the drug and threat induced suffering in California, I feared others could see through me. The truth is I hoped I was hiding it well, but Ryan and Travis both suspected I was using again. I never used before the Sunday ritual, which added another layer of deception. The stakes felt too high, and I needed to hold on to the hope that I would be able to reclaim my freedom from opiates again. I knew I had the ability to abstain from them and had successfully done so for over a year.

My enthusiasm for the film obscured the reality that I was currently using. I so desperately wanted to believe the spiral that had started was just a temporary phase. When the filmmaker reached out to us, a woman contacted us for support simultaneously. At the time, this felt like serendipity. This woman came into our lives, struggling deeply, still using heroin while on methadone. We didn't just see her pain, we saw a possibility. This was a chance to offer her what had saved me and was a chance, to prove that it wasn't just a one-time miracle. And maybe, I could have another miracle too.

We believed we could support her through connection, accountability, and presence. In hindsight, we were out of our depth. Good intentions do not substitute for capacity, and we were learning that lesson too late. Each new alteration changed the dynamic of the ritual.

Looking back, it was a kind of madness I couldn't see from inside it. The ritual we created was fragile, deeply personal, and almost impossible to explain, let alone recreate for someone else, especially someone still caught in the daily cycle of heroin and methadone. We stepped forward anyway, believing that intention and compassion were enough. They weren't.

The filmmaker documented her coming to the group for the first time. I had been hopeful that a documentary would be a viable platform to capture the potential of the ritual, but the documentary medium changed everything. Control slipped away quietly, almost imperceptibly. Decisions were no longer ours alone; the process introduced timelines, expectations, framing, and pressure we were not prepared for.

As the filming continued, the pressure for success mounted. The responsibility blurred. The ritual, once private, protected, and sacred, was now exposed. What had been a space for honesty slowly became something else. I felt myself destabilizing. What had begun as a relapse didn't stay contained for long. It spread slowly at first, then all at once, until it consumed everything I had managed to build. The structure that the ritual had provided before the California nightmare, the fragile sense of direction I thought I still held onto, all of it gave way. The most painful part wasn't that I was using again. It was how the story was told publicly.

When the film was finished, it captured almost none of the depth, care, or value that had existed in that space, not for the woman we were trying to help, and not for the work we had been doing together. And at the end of the film, a line appeared on the screen: "Rory is using again." That was it. No context. No reckoning. No sense of what had been held or lost.

Inviting a filmmaker into what had been a sacred ritual was a mistake. Not because stories shouldn't be told, but because that space hadn't been built to withstand exposure, and we paid for it. The ritual dissolved, the structure collapsed, and I returned to the thing I knew how to reach for when something meaningful broke. My opiate spiral got so bad that I was advised to get back on methadone again, and so I did. The year that followed was the most difficult and disorienting stretch of my life. Eventually, my behavior got so destructive that my parents asked me to leave their house.

There was a particular kind of emptiness that followed. Not anger, not even sadness at first, just a hollow recognition that I had crossed a line I couldn't step back over. I didn't argue. Part of me understood. Another part of me had already started drifting away from myself. I moved in with my girlfriend at the time and stayed with her for a year, existing more than living. When she eventually left and moved across the country, I was left behind in more ways than one. After that, things unraveled quickly.

I rented an apartment for three months, and during that time I smoked more crack than I ever thought was possible. I impulsively sold my car. I took all of that money and spent it on crack. After the California trip, every time I took stimulants, including crack, I experienced paranoid delusions. I would immediately feel euphoria, which then gave way to unrelenting paranoia. One night a few friends and I smoked $1k worth of crack, but the binge went on for months. Throughout these crack-binged months, I called 911 dozens of times hoping that police presence would deter the delusional threats. Eventually, the police stopped responding to my ongoing calls.

Those months felt like a lifetime compressed into something unrecognizable. Days bleeding into nights, reality thinning out at the edges. I was in and out of rehab three times in this period alone. This is about the time that I deleted all of the recorded podcasts off our channel because of the state of mind I was in.

When my housing fell apart, I ended up in a converted hotel. One of those places repurposed into housing for people who had nowhere else to go. I had a room of my own, which, in some strange way, felt like a small victory, but nothing had really changed. The using continued. The cycle stayed intact.

Then, somehow, in the middle of all of that, I met Katie. With her, something shifted, not all at once, not enough to fix everything. Enough to introduce the possibility that maybe, just maybe, this wasn't the end of my story.

Chapter 17

Meeting Katie

The true end of the spiral, the moment everything in me finally changed, came later, after I met Katie. When she entered my life, I was still using, still lying, still doing what addicts do best, pulling reality over myself like a blanket full of holes and pretending it was enough.

I loved her, truly, but I wasn't capable of loving her well. My need for opiates was still louder than my need for connection. The spiral didn't stop when she arrived. In some ways it intensified because now there was someone real to lose.

Katie shared my interest in plant medicine healing and supporting alternative perspectives in mental health. Katie was dedicated to finding a solution to my addiction. She and I had been researching ibogaine for months.

One night I had pushed her beyond her limit. She drove me, high and hopeless, to my parents' house because she couldn't hold me up anymore. I remember lying on the bed in my old room, sweating, withdrawn, drifting, while voices murmured outside the door. I remember the way Katie's voice shook when she talked with my parents about ibogaine.

The way my mother listened as if she already knew the answer. Katie left that night unsure if she'd ever come back, and I couldn't blame her. As she walked toward the door, my mother said the sentence that changed everything. "Okay, Katie. I will pay for Rory to go to Mexico to get the ibogaine treatment." It was a declaration, a lifeline, a line in the sand.

I needed to prepare my body for this process. Before Mexico, I had to be off methadone, again. Ibogaine cannot be taken with methadone in the body, but it can be taken with short-acting opiates still in the body. The heart risks alone are too high on methadone. Methadone typically takes 2-4 weeks to leave the body; for me, it took 31 days. If I had not been on methadone, this process would have been a hell of a lot easier.

The truth is, I wasn't the man who confronted the methadone doctor years earlier. I didn't feel invincible now. I felt worn out, faded, and uncertain. I wanted to believe it was possible to get off methadone again. I wanted to believe I still had enough inside me to fight. Even then, I knew I had to descend one more time, before ibogaine could pull me out. Again, intentionally, with a plan, and with someone willing to enter into hell with me. Her name was Katie. Katie and I designed the only plan that could work.

The Plan: Safe Supply in Canada, short-acting opiates, something unavailable for addicts in the United States.

- Find a doctor, who was willing to prescribe short acting opiates, a nearly impossible task.

- Go to Canada and stay until the methadone cleared my system.

- Switch from methadone to short-acting opiate pills.

- Fly straight to Mexico for ibogaine treatment.

Before Katie and I found a doctor that was willing to help, we called a few different doctors in Vermont, and they were all unable to help me with this plan. One of the doctors we spoke to told us about the Drug Addiction Treatment Act of 2000 (DATA 2000), which primarily restricts how doctors can use opioids to treat addiction. The law only permits the use of FDA-approved Schedule III-V narcotics for addiction treatment (e.g., Buprenorphine/Naloxone), making it illegal for doctors without a specific exemption to prescribe other opioids (like methadone, oxycodone, Dilaudid, and morphine, which are Schedule II). Suboxone/buprenorphine wasn't a solution because it was another long-acting opioid medication just like methadone. Regardless of this DATA 2000 act, we were hopeful that an exception would be made since this was the stepping stone I needed to get to ibogaine. We were told by a number of doctors that was impossible.

After extensive searching, we asked a Canadian doctor Katie had met at a conference, Dr. Andrew Bui-Nguyen. We had a number of calls with Andrew to thoughtfully discuss the risks and safety protocol. The risk of me coming off methadone and switching to short-acting opiates without a safe supply was almost certain death because the heroin supply in Vermont is now almost strictly fentanyl and xylazine. Andrew understood this. It was the only chance left. He agreed to go on this journey with me, so Katie and I went to Canada. After we arrived in Canada, we settled into an Airbnb. I ingested my last dose of methadone. Katie and I went to the doctor's office together. Unlike going into any addiction specialist's office before, Andrew was going to intentionally prescribe me short-acting opiates. He wrote me a prescription and I got it filled at the pharmacy nearby.

Katie went back to the Airbnb with me, and I took the opiates. For the next three weeks the Airbnb became our temporary home and war bunker, our classroom in suffering. For three and a half weeks, methadone drained out of my body like poison. We didn't anticipate how prevalent the crack use would be in downtown Montreal. It was a temptation that we were not expecting in the plan. Methadone withdrawals weren't a wave, they were a tide that never receded, and what made matters worse, I was smoking crack every day throughout the entire detox.

The opiates from the safe supply helped with the detox, but they didn't save me. My tolerance to opiates was so high that they didn't quell the physical dependency completely. It was Katie who stayed and held the line. Katie who watched me sweat, shake, bargain, regress, and fight. It was hell for me, but it was a different kind of hell for her. Katie carried me through the moments I could not carry myself. She cooked, monitored me, researched, stayed awake with me, and sat in silence when I was too mentally raw to speak. Most people never witness addiction so intensely, even fewer stay. She did. Not because I made it easy, but because in her eyes there was something in me that was worth saving, and she refused to let the world take me.

On the day of my flight from Montreal to Cancun, I packed my bags. I was ready, as ready as a drowning man when he sees a rope. Walking toward the Uber, ten Canadian dollars in my hand, I saw him, a crack-user on the corner, familiar in the worst way. Addiction has one last rule, it always tries once more. A man with what I thought I wanted. He saw the money, I saw the opportunity. My addicted brain flared up. One more time, that's the lie addicts believe more than any other. I stepped toward him. One step closer. One exchange away. He asked for the money first. A classic trick. I almost fell for it. Then I heard Katie's voice, furious and panicked. She sprinted toward us from around the corner, shouting: "No! No! No! Get the fuck away from him!" I truly wasn't sure if she was yelling at me or the crack-user. It didn't matter. Her voice cut through the fog, the craving, and the last thread of my self-deception. She intervened like someone trying to save a man from being dragged into a river. Something snapped, something surrendered, I backed away. It was the last time crack ever came close enough to speak to me, and it has been silent ever since.

I got into the Uber, let the door close, felt the car pull forward, and that was it. Canada behind me. Katie behind me. The drugs behind me. I boarded the plane, exhausted, shaking, but alive.

Chapter 18

Ibogaine Reset

The plane touched down in Mexico just before sunset. The sky was the color of cooling embers, the half-light between day and night when everything looks like it's holding its breath. I was exhausted. I was fragile, but I was there. For the first time in years, I wasn't running toward a high or away from a consequence. I was walking toward myself.

The ibogaine center wasn't a hospital, but it wasn't a retreat either. It felt like a threshold, a place designed for crossing. I gave them what was left of my prescriptions. They checked my vitals and asked about my last doses. I still had just under a week before the methadone was completely out of my body, so they gave me short-acting opiates until I had a clean urinalysis from methadone. They listened carefully when I explained the month-long descent I had just survived in Canada. The staff had seen every version of addiction, every collapse, and every resurrection.

They listened to me differently, not because I was special, but because they could tell I was right on the edge. I was the rare kind of patient who was already halfway through the transformation, before the medicine even touched my tongue. I wasn't naïve. I knew ibogaine wasn't magic. I also knew it was my last chance to interrupt a cycle that had almost killed me multiple times.

When they handed me the capsule, that unassuming piece of plant-encoded intelligence, I felt afraid, but I knew what I had to do. I swallowed it with water. Laid back in my bed, closed my eyes, and waited. Ibogaine was a different experience than other plant medicines I've taken. It didn't warm or soften or drift me away. It arrived like a reckoning. My heartbeat reverberated through my entire body, slow, heavy, and deliberate. As if something was knocking from the inside.

Then the memories began, not as images, but as rooms, places in myself I had walled off for years. My mother crying . . . my father's worry disguised as stillness . . . heroin . . . the overdose when my brother found me in an impossible blue . . . Hunter's absence . . . California . . . a hospital curtain I thought hid a gunman . . . Katie's voice on the corner in Canada. Not one memory arrived alone; each came with the emotion that I refused to feel in real time. Grief, fear, shame, love, recognition, and responsibility. Ibogaine didn't let me passively observe my life. It made me attend to it.

There's a point in an ibogaine journey when the medicine stops showing you your life and begins showing you your patterns - the loops, the justifications, the emotional and subconscious architecture of addiction. I watched how every relapse was built from the same blueprint. How Heroin had always offered me an identity, when I couldn't locate my own, how silence became my hiding place, how fear disguised itself as detachment, and how I survived by shrinking. Then something happened that the medicine couldn't force but sometimes allows.

I forgave myself, not in a sentimental way, but in a structural way. The kind of forgiveness that rearranges a life. The kind that says: "I understand why I did what I did, and I choose differently now." When the visions faded, the weight in my body shifted. Opiates were gone, not masked, gone. My physical dependency and withdrawals were completely abolished, a unique feature of ibogaine. The chains my brain had been wrapped in for over a decade, simply weren't there. Most people don't understand what that means. It's not euphoria, it's not clarity, it's silence. My nervous system felt free. The staff saw it before I felt it, the small change in my posture, the way my breathing deepened, the way my eyes didn't dart, shield or search. I wasn't cured, I wasn't finished, but I was reset. No heroin. No methadone. No opiate pull left in my body. For the first time in years, I woke up as the unmedicated version of myself. Truthfully, this felt like the first version of me before I ever touched drugs.

Twenty-four hours after the dose, they brought me food. I barely touched it. They asked how I felt. I didn't have language yet. So I walked outside, into air that felt strangely new. The sky didn't look symbolic, like people often describe after a psychedelic experience. It didn't glow or pulse. It didn't "mean" anything. It was just the sky. Somehow, that was the miracle. My senses weren't chasing anything. My body wasn't negotiating anything. My mind wasn't bargaining with a needle or a pill. I was simply there, present, alive, undivided.

When I boarded the plane going home, I was a different man than the man who had boarded the plane to Mexico. I wasn't the addict. I wasn't the runaway. I wasn't the martyr in waiting. I was the man who had come back from annihilation with both eyes open. I was the man who survived the descent, and now had to face the return. Because transformation isn't the medicine. It's what you do with yourself, after the medicine ends. My rebuilding, sense of responsibility, and identity were just beginning.

Beond, the clinic in Mexico, deserves an entire section in this book. I can't say enough, and I can't thank them enough. My life will forever be changed by what happened there. Gratitude is the only language I have for it. This place was more than a treatment center. It was an initiation to a new life. Beond was a space held with intention, discipline, and care, where I was allowed to step outside the patterns that had defined me and be seen not as a problem to be fixed, but as a human being worth guiding back to himself. It gave me a reference point for what alignment feels like and for what truth sounds like when it's finally quiet enough to hear. That is why it belongs here, not as a footnote in recovery, but as a chapter about becoming.

Beond

I didn't go to Mexico looking for insight. I had enough insight to last a lifetime. I went because my body hadn't caught up to the truth yet. Beond was the place where that disconnect finally ended.

Beond felt calm, sterile, clinical, partially medical in a way that immediately made me feel safe. There was nothing chaotic or indulgent about it. No theatrical spirituality. No performative comfort. The floors were clean, the rooms were quiet, and the staff moved with the kind of precision that told me this place took responsibility seriously. What unsettled me wasn't fear, it was the opposite. Beond felt like a wellness center. For most people, that would have been reassuring. For me, it meant I had almost no excuses left. Beond felt clean, clear, and inescapably earnest. I knew, even on arrival, that confrontation was waiting, and that I wouldn't be able to blame the environment when it came.

Part of me hoped the experience would resolve something for me without requiring my participation. That ibogaine would fix the confrontation I had been avoiding. I didn't know yet how thoroughly that hope would be dismantled. The staff stayed mostly neutral, which I appreciated. They reassured me when reassurance was necessary, but they didn't rush in to rescue me from discomfort. They let me struggle. I never felt evaluated or judged. I felt held, and there's an important difference between the two. The warmth of the Mexican nurses and doctors, their affection and grounded presence, combined with the fact that I was far from home, gave the whole place an added gravity. This wasn't symbolic work. This was real.

When the ibogaine took hold, it didn't offer me visions or revelations in the way I expected. It took things away . . . first control . . . then time . . . then language . . . then identity . . . and then the anguish of the memories. Each loss arrived in order, as if something methodical was dismantling the structures I'd relied on to explain myself to myself. There was no bargaining with it.

The moment I wanted it to stop the most didn't come during the peak. It came the day after the flood dose, on what they call the "grey day." I cried and cried. I called my loved ones and cried. Not because I was afraid of what I'd seen, but because I knew I wouldn't have access to the same coping mechanisms anymore. Not just opiates, but the thought patterns, the rationalizations, the stories I told myself to avoid responsibility. They were gone, and their absence was unbearable.

In the experience, I encountered myself, my death, and my family. I felt the weight of humanity and questioned how to make things better rather than merely survive. None of it came with instruction. It wasn't comforting. It was heavy. The day after the ibogaine flood was the most physically, emotionally, and existentially unpleasant experience I had at Beond. There was no relief in it. No insight to cling to. What didn't survive that day was a belief I hadn't realized I was still carrying: the need for something external, beyond my own mind, body, or will, to survive this world. When it was over, I felt empty and raw. The relief I sought didn't come for a long time. I realize now how much my life has been shaped by the search for it.

My girlfriend, Katie, had flown down to Mexico and met me at the clinic the same day I was discharged. She immediately congratulated me. She was genuinely excited. At the time, it felt false, like I hadn't earned it. All I had done was take a substance and come out feeling more stripped than ever. As I write this, two years later, I understand why she celebrated. She was responding to something I couldn't feel yet. That the plan we created was now complete, and I was starting a new life.

What followed scared me more than anything that came before: the possibility of relapse or regression, the fear that I wouldn't keep moving forward, that I'd return to excuses, that the momentum would collapse and would once again take over. But slowly, over time, almost imperceptibly, that fear loosened its grip. Today, it no longer governs me. The healing came later. Beond wasn't the end. It was the moment the lies stopped working.

When I left Beond, there was no sense of completion, only the uncomfortable awareness that something irreversible had begun. The stripping was over, but nothing had replaced what was taken away. There were no instructions. What remained was a life waiting to be lived without anesthesia or excuses. The question was no longer what would save me, but could I uphold the daily weight of responsibility that now had no buffer.

Before Beond, I had been to rehab over ten times. Walking into those places was always accompanied by a strange sense of relief, not because I was ready to change, but because responsibility temporarily softened at the door. The language sounded right. The intentions were good, but something in me knew almost immediately whether the structure would hold. Often, it did not.

Some rehabs felt symbolic rather than serious, where the philosophy collapsed under scrutiny. Rules were inconsistently enforced. Accountability was uneven. There was always a way to hide, behind group language, behind diagnoses, behind the performance of insight. I learned how to speak recovery fluently without having to live it. I learned how to survive the environment without being changed by it. What Beond lacked, and what made it different, was illusion.

There was no sense that I was being saved. No pressure to feel hopeful. No softening of consequence. The medical seriousness removed the possibility of pretending. The neutrality of the staff didn't allow me to externalize responsibility, and the structure didn't invite interpretation. It simply existed, firm, clear, and unavoidable.

In rehab, I often felt protected from myself. At Beond, I was protected enough to face myself. That distinction matters. Rehab gave me language. Beond took language away. Rehab offered time. Beond demanded honesty.

I don't write this to dismiss one or elevate the other. For some people, rehab is lifesaving. For me, it wasn't enough. I needed a container that didn't negotiate with my intelligence, my charm, or my capacity to explain myself out of consequence. After Beond, I didn't need more insight. I needed a way to live.

In the return to my disillusioned life, I learned that it is not just a moment. It's a practice. It's waking up and choosing not to lie. It's staying present when it would be easier to disappear. It's enduring the cost of love and responsibility. It's accepting that freedom isn't the absence of constraint, it's the willingness to stay disciplined when distraction beckons.

It has now been two years since I went to Beond, and my life no longer resembles the one I was living before. In the most literal sense, I have remained off methadone, free from the physical dependency that once governed my body, and untouched by cocaine and crack. Opiates would appear a few more times in the six months following my return home from Beond, before my final confrontation with them, which ultimately led to their disappearance from my life.

I learned early on that truth doesn't spread through instruction. It spreads through story. One person speaking honestly creates space for another to do the same. That is how change moves through a community, person to person, story by story.

I think that's part of why I'm telling this story now. Not because my experience is unique, but because it isn't. Because I've sat in enough rooms, listening to enough lives, to know that when one person tells the truth clearly, it opens a door for others to do the same.

As I write this, the impact is still unfolding. Ibogaine gave me something no therapy, spiritual practice, or drug ever had. My experience at Beond replaced the chaos in my life with stability, and compulsion with choice. The man writing these words is living proof that something real happened there.

Chapter 19

The Death of Heroin

Part of me believed ibogaine would be the end of my addiction. In many ways, it was. Physically, it stripped me of my desire for opiates, but something within me remained. Ibogaine left me no longer craving heroin. It left me with a need for closure and an understanding of why I began using heroin in the first place. That belief led to the desire for a "last time" use.

Ibogaine is known to eliminate opioid tolerance, making any return to use significantly more dangerous by increasing the risk of overdose.

I wanted to find meaning in the thing that once controlled me. I wasn't being pulled by a craving to use, I was being pulled by the desire for closure. After ibogaine, my relationship with opiates changed. With the physical dependency gone, I had the opportunity to explore why I had developed the relationship with heroin in the first place. I wanted to use one more time to investigate how that relationship changed, but I knew the only heroin I could get in Vermont was laced with fentanyl.

I sought heroin three times after ibogaine but received fentanyl instead. I overdosed all three times. None of these experiences led to any clarity on why I had used heroin in the first place or the relationship I had with it.

I feel it's important to highlight this because ibogaine isn't a cure-all. Ibogaine significantly reduces physical dependency and withdrawal, which gives people an opportunity to break free from the cycle of addiction. Ibogaine also demands integration. Integration is an essential part of psychedelic experiences. Ibogaine asked me to investigate why I was using opiates in the first place, and I didn't know how to integrate this question without using again. Ryan and my parents vehemently opposed it; they had seen this a hundred times before, as a justification to return to the opiates.

I didn't want to return to the cycle, but I couldn't let go of the desire of wanting to use a "last time." It consumed me. I tried to articulate why this felt so critical to me, yet it was hard for other people to understand. Honestly, it was hard for me to understand. How would this break the cycle? How would this not lead to continued use? Katie simply saw what I couldn't deny anymore. I needed a final confrontation, with the last fragment of myself that still believed opiates had anything left to offer.

Over the next few months, I talked with Katie and my family about my desire to have a "last time" use. I felt two opposite truths at once. I didn't want opiates, but I needed to end my relationship with them consciously. They were insistent that I only do so safely, and the only way to do this safely was to go back to Canada. So we pitched it - it was a long shot - but we reached out to Dr. Andrew and told him the situation that I was in.

Andrew sympathized, and he asked me why I wasn't focusing more on integrating the ibogaine. I told him ibogaine felt almost complete, but without the "last time" closure, it felt incomplete. I told him about the overdoses after ibogaine. We talked about how a "last time" without an opportunity for extensive processing would be misguided. He challenged me to think about my use differently, but he accepted that I identified that I needed this. He listened to me.

We talked about a plan for me to take psilocybin to engage this entire process of a "last time" like a ceremony. I would have two days of safe supply, with intentional therapy, and then I could have a guided medical psilocybin session. Andrew introduced us to his colleague, Fred, who is a psychedelic guide. Andrew, Fred, Katie, my parents, and I designed the plan together. We picked an Airbnb that would be conducive to the experience. It was collaborative and it was empowering. For the first time in my life, people wanted to sit with me while I used opiates without shame and without judgement. This time, however, I wasn't bargaining. I wasn't hiding. I was preparing for a funeral. A last goodbye.

The plan was simple. I would return to Canada. I would receive a controlled, safe supply of short-acting opiates. I would have my "last time," not in secrecy but in full accountability. Forty-eight hours after arrival, I would take seven grams of psilocybin, a dose designed not to heal addiction, but to confront its psychological root. It was, in every sense, the last chapter of a story that had gone on too long. It wasn't reckless. It wasn't impulsive. It wasn't a relapse disguised as therapy. It was intentional intervention, a structured, medically supervised, psychologically informed ending.

So, Katie and I went to Canada. Upon arriving, Andrew and Fred were set up in the Airbnb and waiting for us. Andrew had called the scripts into the pharmacy, and we walked across the street to pick them up. Andrew prescribed the medication with the same seriousness he had shown when he helped transition me off methadone. Fred left to get safe injection supplies because I knew that I wanted to inject, something that I didn't feel that I could do in Vermont, due to the unpredictability of the drug supply and prevalence of fentanyl. And then I went through my process; the unhealthy ritual that had consumed me for years was actually now a part of a real ritual that preceded ceremony. They circled around me, symbolically holding me, while I injected without shame, and then we talked. We talked about how I felt, why I felt so compelled to use and why I felt heroin was still calling me.

The use didn't bring pleasure or relief. It genuinely felt different than every other time I used opiates before, because it was. Ibogaine forced me to realize that my sober self was my optimal self, a tough truth to accept for someone whose entire life had been dictated by the belief that I needed substances to survive. This last use brought understanding and closure. In that rare moment of intentional, guided use, I was able to experience the opiate no longer in the shadow, but fully seen. Legally sanctioned and surrounded by trusted allies, I wasn't driven by compulsion, but by a deep intent to understand the role it had played in my life and examine why I had held so closely to the idea of a "last time."

I questioned: Did I need to give something up to get there or did I need to accept something? Perhaps it was both a letting go and an accepting? Katie and I talked a lot about how substances can serve people, that people often use substances as a means to survive intense feelings they are struggling to accept or let go of. I finally didn't feel that I was doing something wrong, this was legal, accepted, and guided. It was an opportunity to honor heroin and the role it had served in my life and to say goodbye. Using the opiates this time, I didn't experience the same relief I always had in the past. At some point, finally, *I thought*: "I am done with this."

Then came the medicine that would seal the acceptance. Psilocybin is a teacher, not a rescuer. It reveals. Seven grams did not ask me who I was, it showed me. It disillusioned me from what I thought heroin was. As the journey began, I felt ibogaine's work rising to meet it, two medicines from two different continents communicating in my bloodstream. I saw the architecture of my addiction laid bare, the patterns, the emotional signatures, the survival strategies, the identity scaffolding, the unconscious contracts, the lies I told myself to stay alive, the lies I told others to stay hidden, the child inside me who believed pain made me valuable, the man who believed destruction made him strong, and the soul that believed it was unworthy of peace.

Then, came a rupture: A moment when the medicine showed me my life as if I were already dead, a vision not of fear, but of absolute futility. Then came the release. Finally, *I felt*: "I am done with this." I found the meaning that I was searching for. For the first time in my adult life, the part of my identity that clung to opiates let go. Not because it was forced but because it was understood. I watched the identity of "heroin user" unravel itself like an old thread and fall away. I emerged without cravings, without desire, without the echo, and most importantly without the identity.

What happened in that room was grace, but it was also a mirror. The doctor's steadiness, Katie's unwavering presence, the way they held me when I could not hold myself. Those were not powers I was meant to borrow forever. They were examples. Eventually, no matter how profound the intervention or how loving the support, the responsibility returns to me. There comes a point when the hands that steady us must become our own. When the voice that reminds us to breathe must rise from our own soul.

The final step was not another treatment. It was the decision to show up for myself with the same devotion others had shown me, and to never abandon that responsibility again.

I carry a deep reverence for Andrew and the way he guided me through that chapter of my life. The level of compassion, trust, and empathy he showed me was unlike anything I had ever experienced in a medical setting. He didn't just see my addiction; he saw me, and more importantly, he trusted me in moments when I didn't fully trust myself. If it weren't for his presence, I have no doubt I would still be caught in that cycle. What stands out most is not just that he helped me transition away from methadone in a way that felt safe and humane; but that even after everything, after ibogaine, after the progress I had made, he met me again with that same steadiness. In a space where most would have drawn a hard line, he responded with discernment instead of judgment. Not because he believed in the idea of one "last time," but because he listened to me well enough to know what I needed in that moment. That kind of care is rare, and it changed the trajectory of my life.

The addict in America has to hide his or her use out of fear of judgment and out of fear of imprisonment. The behavior is deemed by society as bad and wrong, creating shame. That shame perpetuates the disease, creating a vicious cycle. The deeper someone falls, the more they are forced into secrecy, and the more that secrecy feeds the very thing they are trying to escape.

That cycle is not broken by punishment. It is not broken by isolation. It is not broken by forcing someone to hide. One way to break free is by offering something our current medical system does not allow and something our country does not yet accept: allowance.

Allowance for honesty, so that we don't have to hide who we are. Allowance for safe and supervised drug use, preventing overdose and death. Allowance for people to be met where they actually are, not where we wish they would be.

When I took the Dilaudid, during my last use, I was not hiding. I was not looking over my shoulder. I was not afraid of being judged, arrested, or cast out. I was held in a space with intention and a plan, that allowed me to confront myself fully, without shame, without secrecy, without the constant threat that defines addiction in America. That difference is everything, because healing cannot happen in hiding. It cannot happen under threat. And it cannot happen in a system that punishes the very people it claims to help.

Chapter 20

The Work that Happened Quietly

Some of the most important work of my recovery didn't happen in ceremonies or moments of revelation. It happened in a quiet office, one conversation at a time. For the past seven years, I've been in psychotherapy. Unlike the rituals or plant medicine ceremonies, therapy never felt dramatic or revelatory. There were no visions, and no sudden breakthroughs that reshaped everything overnight. Often it felt slow, sometimes frustrating, and occasionally, I wondered if anything was really changing at all.

When I first told my therapist about ayahuasca, it was after my first experience with it. He had never heard of it before. I explained that it was a psychedelic used ceremonially in parts of South America, and that people believed it had therapeutic value. From his perspective, it was difficult to evaluate. His work as a psychoanalytic therapist is grounded in observing change through patterns of thought, behavior, and emotional responses over time. From his perspective, one powerful experience alone doesn't necessarily demonstrate lasting transformation.

Six months later, when I had come off methadone, he began to notice a difference in me. Something about the way I spoke, the way I thought about my life, had shifted. When I relapsed and returned to methadone, his professional conclusion was that whatever effect the ayahuasca experience had, it did not produce stable change without regression. And in some ways, he was right.

What was harder to see from the outside was that something inside me had still changed. Even after my relapse, the way I understood myself and my life was no longer quite the same. Years later, when I spoke to him about this, he agreed that something had shifted internally. What he didn't see at the time was enough consistency to call it lasting recovery. For lasting recovery, he believed I needed to show up to therapy sober and engaged over time. Looking back now, I think he was right about that too.

Two years ago, when I told him about ibogaine, he was once again confronted with something outside the framework of traditional therapy. After the ibogaine experience, I began committing to therapy more consistently than I ever had before. Week after week I showed up and began doing the real work of examining my thoughts, my patterns, and the ways I had learned to survive the world. With that investment, therapy began to pay off.

Ibogaine did not replace therapy, but it made me finally ready for it. Plant medicines often create moments of revelation. Therapy creates habits of understanding. My life began to change when both of those things started working together.

The long relationship with my therapist remains deeply important to me. He witnessed the entire arc of my life during those years of addiction, the searching, the ceremonies, the relapses, and the slow rebuilding that followed.

Today I look forward to those sessions in a way I never did before. I get more out of them now than I ever have. Looking back, it's clear that while the breakthroughs may have come in moments, much of the real healing had been quietly unfolding there all along.

Over the years, my therapist has witnessed versions of me that few people ever saw. He knew me when addiction felt inevitable, when hope felt distant, and when I was still searching for something I didn't yet understand. He watched me stumble, relapse, question myself, and slowly begin to change. If the ceremonies revealed who I could become, therapy helped me understand how to live as that person.

And now, the work finally feels like it belongs to me.

PART V

THE RETURN

Chapter 21

Integration - The Magic

Upon my return home from Montreal, I was different. The responsibility in my choices wasn't performative. The ayahuasca awakening was now accessible for me to integrate. The grief wasn't drowning me any longer, and my trauma was transformed.

As the year passed, I met parts of myself I hadn't known in years, or maybe I had never known them at all. I met the man who could feel emotion before reacting and the man who could sit in discomfort without escaping. This was the transformation. Pieces of me that had been buried under trauma, drugs, and defense mechanisms.

Transformation didn't arrive all at once. It arrived in layers over years. Ayahuasca removed the veil, the ritual stabilized the mind, ibogaine reset the body, responsibility matured the soul, and psilocybin finalized the death of opiates. Ryan and Katie held the mirror through every stage of becoming.

The integration of these events led to a cumulative truth. A truth that now lives in me and guides me. My identity is something I choose intentionally. I am no longer surviving my life. *I am living it.*

For nearly a decade, I woke up to the same feeling every morning, a desire to get drugs. A monumental moment occurred when I woke up and my first thought wasn't to go get drugs, it was to make breakfast. To anyone else, an ordinary moment, but to me this was a milestone.

My integration illuminated: suffering is not failure or weakness, it's information. It taught: pain is not the enemy, pain is the messenger. The only true enemy is avoidance. Every piece of suffering carries instruction. I had to learn to integrate all the parts of myself.

For a long time, I believed that something behind me had been better than what was in front of me. There was a version of the past I kept returning to in my mind, a time that felt more wondrous and alive. When the present became heavy or painful, my instinct was to turn backwards, convinced that if I could just reach that place again, something in me would settle. What I didn't understand then was that the place I was chasing had never actually existed the way I remembered it. Memory is not an archive, it's a storyteller. It edits and softens edges. It removes the boredom, the fear, the dissatisfaction that was always there, and leaves behind a distilled feeling. The past becomes a symbol rather than a reality, a story we tell ourselves about who we were before things went wrong.

During my addiction, this illusion became fuel. I wasn't just using to escape pain, I was using to return to that moment. Every substance carried the promise of getting me back to a feeling I believed I had once known, a sense of ease, belonging, or completeness. I told myself I was chasing relief, but the truth is I was chasing a memory that had been polished into something it never was. The present demanded things of me, the past did not. Escaping gave me the illusion I could live in a false memory. My clarity came through years of repeated confrontations with myself and through plant medicine journeys that stripped the nostalgia of its costume and showed me what was actually underneath it.

What I was really seeking wasn't a time in my past, it was a feeling of alignment. My fixation on a "last time" use was a reflection of this conflict. Once I saw that, the chase lost its power. Recovery, for me, wasn't about reclaiming a lost self. It was about building a part of myself that had never existed before, grounded in reality rather than memory. I had mistaken memory for identity and longing for truth. Letting go of that illusion was the first honest step towards becoming myself. People do not transform alone. I learned this through suffering. Addiction, anger, shame, grandiosity, and fear all end in isolation. Everything that destroys a man does so by convincing him he does not need others, or worse, that others do not want him.

In September of 2025, long after the chaos had quieted and the rituals had taken root, I traveled for a traditional ayahuasca ceremony. It wasn't a rescue mission or a desperate attempt to stop myself from slipping. I wasn't running from anything. I went because I was finally strong enough to listen. To deepen, not to escape.

I laid my mat on the floor of a dim, cedar-scented room. The air hummed with the anticipation that always comes before a ceremony. As I settled in, the man beside me introduced himself with a soft nod.

"My name is Hunter."

There was no reason for this to shake me, but it did, deeply, in a way that bypassed thought and went straight to the soul. I didn't know this man, yet something in me recognized the moment. Not his face or his voice, but the name, and the timing, and the weight of it. "Hunter." The name of the boy who shaped my adolescence, who opened the doorway to addiction, who died too young, the name of the ghost that had followed me through a decade of reckoning; but here, in this room, this time, it didn't feel haunting. It felt like witnessing, a presence, not a shadow.

As the ceremony unfolded, I didn't unravel. I deepened. The medicine didn't tear me open, it opened around me, like a widening field. And all through the ceremony, the presence beside me felt like a message, a reminder, a soft returning to something I had long believed was lost. The deceased people who shaped my story, whether they meant to or not, the ones whose absence forced me into the fire, and the ones whose memories walk beside me, were all present with me when I was finally ready to bear the heaviness of their loss.

When the ceremony closed, I thanked Hunter. He didn't know why. He didn't need to. Maybe he was just a man with a name. Or maybe the universe uses names the way it uses storms and synchronicities, precisely, unmistakably. What mattered was, I left that room with the sense that a circle had closed. That some part of my story had come home. And in that room, in the quiet residue of the ceremony, I felt it clearly: "You made it, Rors. Keep going." And for the first time in a long time, I believed it.

The structure I once needed in weekly rituals has softened into something less glaring but more constant: the rhythm of making coffee in the morning, the pause before opening my emails, the deliberate choice to take a break when work starts to feel too stressful. These small acts have become my anchors, my way of returning to myself without needing to leave my life. Where there used to be distance, there is now presence. I make time each week not for escape, but for connection. Sitting down to dinner with family, being with friends without urgency, and allowing those moments to matter. The work didn't end with the rituals. It became steady, ordinary, and, in its own way, sacred.

Chapter 22

The Ground

For a long time, my relationships with other people were shaped by avoidance more than connection. I used drugs as a way to excuse my behavior and avoid meaningful connection. I would retreat, hide, or push people away before they had the chance to leave me. At times, I even let people down on purpose, testing whether their love could survive my worst behavior, as if betrayal could somehow prove devotion.

Drugs became the perfect accomplice in this pattern. If I used enough, I could convince myself that nothing mattered, including what others thought and who I was becoming. It dulled my awareness, lowered my inhibitions, and gave me something external to blame. Beneath it all, I cared deeply about how I was perceived, but the longer I used, the easier it became to disconnect from that truth. My growing identity reshaped itself around the role of a "drug user," because it felt safer to embody that than to face the weight of expectation, disappointment, and judgment. This may sound ironic, but I decided this gave me more control of the narrative and something specific to blame.

In trying to escape those feelings, I only deepened the cycle. Physical dependence forced me to stay in a pattern that I, at times, didn't want to be in. In the absence of healthy connection, I found consistency in something that could never leave, challenge me, or require growth. Without realizing it, I gave my loyalty, time, and emotional center to the one thing that was always there, the one thing I could trust: heroin. My most consistent and longest relationship in my life was with heroin. I allowed substances to dictate my identity. They became a constant and ever-present excuse to no longer need to be accountable for letting people down, and I let people down a lot. Under the influence, I didn't have to feel the consequences of watching someone be disappointed in me. The edges blurred and responsibility lost meaning.

What I learned with integration is the importance of honesty, expectations, and boundaries. Avoidance of these destroy relationships. I no longer need to disappear to protect myself or to protect others from discomfort. The people who matter remain. Learning to understand that I have disappointed others has been one of the hardest truths of sobriety. For most of my life, I believed my role was to feel and hold everything together, and I was unable to do so. I lost myself under the pressure of this belief. Integration has reaffirmed that my sensitivity was never meant to be hidden. It was meant to guide me. Learning to follow my intuition, without abandoning myself, may be the hardest, and most necessary, part of who I am.

Integrating these experiences led me to realize that transforming my identity isn't about becoming someone new or longing for an old self. I have the same roots. My roots didn't need to change and were never going to change. The integration process led me to feel grounded and steady. It allowed me to grow into myself and become capable of living without constant existential negotiation. Sobriety isn't just the absence of drugs. It's about the presence of self and feeling safe with myself in those moments.

Truth is the beginning of all healing. I need to be honest with myself and with others. Identity for me began the moment I stopped lying to myself and when I started to feel safe being honest with others. It was difficult. That is why my awakening was painful, why the ritual was uncomfortable, and why I could no longer tolerate the artificial confidence of opiates. Truth, once seen, demands to be lived. We can try to resist, but the dissonance cannot be escaped, only repressed.

Awakening came in the presence of my family. The ritual was built by fire with my brother and a friend. Transformation was witnessed by Katie. The substances that facilitated my healing, ayahuasca, ibogaine, and psilocybin, did their work while I was anchored to my to human support systems. My understanding is simple: people heal with connection.

Katie played a crucial role in this stage, not by defining my identity, but by challenging the parts of me that still tried to fragment. She didn't accept my shrinking, self-doubt, avoidance, emotional shortcuts, or narratives of inadequacy. She held me accountable to who I was becoming, instead of who I used to be. Identity is never built alone. It requires relationships, not co-dependence, but reflection. Through Katie's eyes, I saw the man capable of real partnership. Her love didn't shape my identity; it made me responsible to live it.

I am grateful to have support systems that guided me through this journey. None of my healing happened in isolation. My family loved me with a loyalty that defied logic. My mother held the family together. My dad steadied us through the storm. Ryan stayed close through stretches that tested patience, trust, and hope. Not as a rescuer, but as a brother who chose presence when distance would have been easier. He walked beside me through much of the confusion and pain, helping me find my way out and trusting me to do so. His consistency was one of the reasons my return remained possible at all. Their sacrifice and commitment informs the man I am becoming.

Responsibility, to me, is the understanding that my healing does not belong to me alone. That in becoming whole, I carry forward something of theirs as well. I've come to see a healthy community the way I see the ground beneath us: steady, ever-present, yet essential. It holds us, nourishes us, and gives us something to root into when everything else feels uncertain. This is the ground we stand on, and the ground that nurtures us into who we are meant to be, not in isolation, but together.

Chapter 23

The Tree

Most of my life, I lived without anything resembling a creed. Although I had an understanding of values, it was hard to have integrity. I was afraid of what choosing a life path would demand of me. I know now, a creed isn't a slogan we repeat when things are going well. It's a standard we're measured against when they aren't. For most of my life, I wasn't ready to live under that kind of pressure.

What I've come to understand is that a creed isn't something someone can simply teach you. It forms out of consequence and survival. It emerges from the wreckage of who we used to be, from the moments that nearly destroyed us, from the rituals that rebuilt us, and from the people who refused to give up on us. A creed is shaped by what endures the fire.

The purpose of having a creed is to become responsible for the forces within us and to align them. My creed didn't arrive in a single revelation. It accumulated, piece by piece, after responsibility stopped feeling optional. Somewhere along the way, positive patterns became trusted principles.

The first principle is alignment with my body. I need to be aware of my body, nourish it, and exercise. When my mind gets anxious, I breathe, and literally listen to my heartbeat. This principle demands awareness so I am accountable to the choices I make with my body.

The second principle is honesty. It took longer to accept this because it meant acknowledging how much of my life I'd been dishonest. I used to believe honesty meant confession, something I offered after the damage was done. I now understand honesty is a principle that I need to live by. I avoided honesty because I feared its consequences. Over time, a rule emerged that I now live by: speak the truth early, or suffer later.

The third principle is incorporating healthy rituals. Ritual gives structure to insight and instills intention into action. The consistency isn't about discipline; it's about faith. Faith that the actions are meaningful. That they'll lead to healing, growth, and to something larger than the self.

The fourth principle is courage. It requires courage to live honestly, intentionally, and lovingly. Courage rarely looks the way we imagine it will. Courage is telling someone we love them without knowing how it will be received. It's admitting fear instead of hiding behind certainty. It's asking for help when pride tells us not to. It's staying present through a psychedelic storm instead of running back to numbness. It's walking into ibogaine knowing it will dismantle me. It's declining the dealer's hand even when my mind whispers that it wouldn't matter. It took me years to understand that courage isn't the absence of fear; it's how you navigate it.

The fifth principle is love. Love, finally, revealed itself in a form I hadn't understood before. Not romance or sentiment, but presence, witnessing, and commitment. Love is the act of returning to the people who stayed, who refused to give up on me even when I gave them reasons to. Katie showed me that love isn't a reward we earn once we're fixed. It's a mirror that reflects both who we are and who we're capable of becoming. Love doesn't ask for perfection. It asks for responsibility for the impact our presence has on the world around us.

The sixth principle is community. We need to find and have community to heal. We can't heal in isolation. When I was sober and participating in the ritual for the first year, I was healing by surrounding myself with others. We need a community that is understanding, empathetic, and nonjudgmental to support people in getting through challenging times. I believe transformation is possible with the support of others. I also believe that giving of oneself and being in service to the community can be a powerful way to stay connected and sober.

A creed is what forms when someone stops betraying themself. It becomes a compass guiding the next steps. A structure that keeps one present and aware. A reminder, not of who one claims to be, but of who one is choosing to become.

My creed makes me accountable. It's meant to be lived, daily and deliberately. I write it here not to convince you, but as a reminder to myself for when inevitably things get hard. Recovery doesn't mean the end of struggles, it means that when challenges arise I'll be prepared with the tools I've acquired.

Ultimately, the creed is about connection. Connection to oneself, to the present moment, to purpose, to others and to nature. When I step back and look at these principles together, a tree emerges. I am the tree. Through strength and growth, I forged my creed into being. The creed is my trunk, bending just enough to withstand the wind without breaking.

This is the creed I live by now. Not because it's noble, but because it keeps me alive.

Chapter 24

The Forest

This past year, I had moments that defined my journey and connected me to something greater than myself. Moments that made it clear my life was never meant to end where it almost did.

I always believed my story was something to survive, not something to carry forward. Addiction narrowed my world until the only goal was getting through the day. Legacy felt like something reserved for other people. People who had built something stable and worth remembering.

My legacy will be shaped by the choices I make, in the way I respond to pain, in whether I turn toward responsibility or away from it. It's my willingness to be honest about what has happened to me and what I have done, but to not let that define where I am going. It's me choosing to show up fully, even when it's uncomfortable. It's me refusing to reduce my legacy to one moment or action.

I will not let addiction define me. Addiction is not simple. It is not just a failure of will or a lack of discipline. It is pain, disconnection, the environment, biology; and everything we don't want to look at, layered together until it becomes something overwhelmingly suffocating. And when we misunderstand it, we don't just let down ourselves, we let down our families and entire communities. That's part of what I hope this book can challenge.

What saved me wasn't punishment or being told I had to change or face consequences. It was being seen. It was people meeting me where I was, without reducing me to what I had done. It was the rare kind of compassion that doesn't excuse behavior, but also doesn't strip away humanity. That kind of response is not common, but it should be.

If we want things to change, we have to be willing to rethink what recovery looks like. We have to allow space for different paths. We have to recognize that healing doesn't always follow the structure we expect it to. We have to listen to the people who have lived it. There is knowledge in lived experience that is valuable and needs to be embedded into care.

Recovery is not one size fits all. My recovery is not the same as anyone else's. Many people in recovery will criticize my path because I do not live totally drug-abstinent, and I do not condemn drugs as bad. I believe the effects of drugs are dependent on the relationships we create with them. My relationship with opiates is toxic. Therefore, I choose not to use them, but opiates are of critical importance in medical care today. My story highlights that they can also be extremely destructive. We need to challenge our preconceptions of drugs. The fears that we were taught when we were in school only create stigma and perpetuate the issue. Drugs demand our deepest respect. They are powerful and should not be used lightly, but in the right context, they can be forces, not of destruction, but of creation and healing. Part of my story is about learning to respect and utilize substances with intention in a way that enriches my sober life, rather than depending on substances to numb suffering.

I find myself now standing at a point where the past is no longer something I'm trying to escape, but something I'm trying to understand, integrate, and use. I think about what it means to build something that lasts. A conversation that shifts something. A story that makes someone feel less alone. A different way of thinking that opens a door where there wasn't one before. That's the kind of legacy I care about, one that moves toward something meaningful and invites others to do the same.

I don't believe it's my job to save anyone. I do believe it is my responsibility to be honest about what I've lived through and to use it in a way that might help someone else find their footing. Even if it's just enough to make them pause, reconsider, or hold on a little longer. Sometimes, that's all it takes. A moment. A shift. A different perspective. And everything begins to change.

For a long time, I thought change had to come from something outside of me, a breakthrough, a single moment powerful enough to undo everything that came before it; like I'd show up to therapy one day and my therapist would have me all figured out and have the solution as well. What I've learned is that change is slower and more internal than that. It happens in the decisions we make every day.

That's what this past year has shown me. That my life is not defined by where it broke, but by what I choose to build afterward. If there's anything I hope remains after this book, it's this: That no matter how far someone has gone, no matter how lost things may feel, there is still something there worth building, something worth carrying forward, something worth becoming. That is legacy.

Church Street in Burlington is a place I know intimately, one of my old battlefields. Very recently, I met someone there to discuss this book, and it was in that moment that everything felt like it came full circle. The street itself hadn't changed, the same buildings, the same movement, the same struggles playing out beneath the surface. However, something in me was different. I wasn't scanning the crowds looking for the one who might have what I want. I wasn't looking over my shoulder fearing a threat. I was simply walking. In my hands was a manuscript, the story of everything I've lived through. For years, I had come to that street looking for drugs. That day, I returned carrying the story of how I survived them. And in that moment, it became clear: the place hadn't changed, but I had.

I feel hopeful for the future in a way I once couldn't imagine. That hope is what drives the work ahead. Through Cultivating Connections, a non-profit Ryan and I founded, I plan to build something rooted in real human connection, spaces where people can step out of isolation and into something honest, supportive, and grounded. Not a system that forces outcomes, but an environment that allows people to rediscover what matters to them. My goal is to take everything I've lived through and help shape something that can reach others, individuals and families alike, and be part of a broader shift in how we approach healing.

We are all trees in the forest, and sometimes it is hard to see the forest for the trees. I hope my book serves as a way to reach individual trees within our forest, and to begin challenging the shape of the forest itself. The forest is not fixed. It grows, it bends, it adapts, and it becomes something new with every root that chooses a different direction. If even one tree finds light where it once believed there was none, then the forest has already begun to change. And maybe that is where it starts, not all at once, but one life at a time, reshaping the whole.

And it is with this sentiment that I write this, with the hope that this story reaches the people who need it most, individuals still struggling and their families. I also have a deeper hope, that something in my story contributes, even in a small way, to changing the systems that shape treatment for addiction. Healing isn't just personal, it's something we build together. In connection, in community, and in the willingness to meet people where they are. If this story carries anything forward, I hope it is that change is possible, for individuals struggling and for the communities that hold them.

Reflections

Recovery was not made easy for me, and I didn't do it alone. The treatments that ultimately helped me most, ibogaine and psilocybin-assisted healing, were not available where I lived. They were not discussed openly in the clinics I attended. They were not offered by the professionals tasked with keeping me alive. In many settings, they were not even allowed to be spoken about without judgment.

Psychedelic and plant-based therapies remain illegal in much of the United States. Access required leaving the country. It required financial resources I did not have. It required trust in people I had never met. It required navigating stigma, skepticism, and silence within both healthcare and social environments. And it required explaining myself repeatedly to people who assumed I was chasing another high rather than searching for healing.

The irony is not lost on me.

I had legal access to methadone for years. I had access to short-term rehabilitation centers repeatedly. I had access to emergency rooms every time I overdosed. What I did not have easy access to was the kind of intervention that addressed both my body and my sense of self. That does not mean conventional treatments are useless. They kept me alive long enough to find another way, but survival and healing are not the same thing.

I do not present plant medicine as a miracle cure. It did not save me in isolation. What changed my life was the combination of difficult responsibility, ritual discipline, community accountability, structured psychedelic intervention, and committed support from loved ones.

Remove any one of these, and the outcome would have been different.

Recovery should not depend on privilege, geography, or the willingness to navigate stigma. If this book carries any argument at all, it is not that everyone should follow my path. It is that we must expand the conversation.

Addiction is not only a chemical problem. It is an identity fracture. It is a trauma wound. It is a spiritual collapse. Treating it as only one of those things leaves many people circling the same ground.

The world is changing. The way we understand trauma, the way we regard psychedelics, the way we think about responsibility and ritual needs to be explored. I am not a clinician or an evangelist. I am someone who survived long enough to tell the truth about what helped. And if telling that truth makes recovery slightly more possible for someone who feels trapped between silence and stigma, then the distance I had to travel was worth it.

Every return carries the responsibility to leave the path clearer for the next person. Policy change is not just important, it is urgent. The way the medical system in the United States is structured is not built for people like me or people struggling with addiction, trauma, neglect, or abuse. It is built in many ways to profit from suffering, especially from those who still have the means to pay for treatment. But what happens to the ones who don't? What happens to the person who has already lost everything, who cannot afford medical care, cannot access compassionate treatment, and who is legally barred from pursuing the very forms of healing that might save their life?

I was given access to things that most people are denied. I was able to explore holistic healing in ways that, in this country, are often criminalized or dismissed. I was given space to heal through plant medicines that allowed me to confront truths I could not access in ordinary consciousness. I was given safe supply that removed the constant threat of death from an unpredictable drug supply. I was supported by people who had lived it; through peer support that offered not just guidance, but understanding at a level no clinical model can replicate.

None of this should be rare, illegal, or reserved for the few. And yet, it is. People are not dying because recovery is impossible. People are dying because access is. We have built a system that criminalizes survival while restricting the very tools that make healing possible. We tell people to get better, but we deny them the means to do so safely, legally, and with dignity. This has to change.

We need to move beyond stigma and into understanding. We need laws that reflect reality, not fear. We need safe, regulated supply instead of a toxic and lethal street market. We need the responsible integration of plant medicines into therapeutic spaces. We need to recognize peer support not as secondary, but as essential. This is not about ideology. This is about life and death.

Without these things, I would not be here, and there are countless others who never had the chance. The question is no longer whether these approaches have value. The question is how long we are willing to wait, and how many more lives we are willing to lose, before we allow them to be accepted as usual forms of treatment.

A special thanks to -

Ryan Van Tuinen - my brother, whose loyalty, honesty, and steady presence has shaped more of this journey than words can capture

Katie - the love who found me in my darkest season and never let go; your devotion to healing others through peer support is changing the world

My Parents - Craig and Carol Van Tuinen, whose love remained constant through chaos, and whose presence shaped more of my path than I understood at the time

To My Therapist - for seven years of steady guidance and for the work that often goes unseen but changes everything

Dr. Andrew Bui-Nguyen - whose compassionate care not only saved my life but helped me finally release the last whisper of addiction

Tom Feegel and Talia Eisenberg - for helping create the conditions in which lasting change could take root

Hunter - whose love and loss shaped me in ways I am still discovering

~ And to the part of me that refused to disappear ~

*And a very special thanks to the Moody Blues,
Emancipator, and Illenium for inspiring me to put
words to my story*

www.ingramcontent.com/pod-product-compliance
Lightning Source LLC
Chambersburg PA
CBHW071439130726
47997CB00006B/2158